THE AGE OF HEROES

The Incredible World of Telugu Cinema

Mukesh Manjunath

HarperCollins *Publishers* India

First published in India by HarperCollins *Publishers* 2024
4th Floor, Tower A, Building No. 10, DLF Cyber City,
DLF Phase II, Gurugram, Haryana – 122002
www.harpercollins.co.in

2 4 6 8 10 9 7 5 3 1

P-ISBN: 978-93-90327-30-0
E-ISBN: 978-93-90327-31-7

Typeset in 11.5/15 Adobe Jenson Pro (OTF) at
Manipal Technologies Limited, Manipal

Printed and bound at
Thomson Press (India) Ltd

To
Vibhu,
Manasa,
Vamsi,
And all my English and Telugu teachers
for encouraging me to read, write and rewrite.

Contents

1

Introduction

'Katurian: I'm not trying to say anything at all! That's my whole thing.'

— Martin McDonagh, *The Pillowman*

You've opened to this page, unsure of whether to read this book or not. It sits on your palm like a bird about to take off. You probably have many questions and concerns.

Why should I read this book?
I have never watched a Telugu film.
I don't know enough. Will I understand?

Forget that you are holding a book. Imagine, instead, that you have walked into a theatre, with the apprehension reserved for a blind date. The seats are plush. The popcorn is next to you. You are comfortable. The national anthem is over, and the film begins.

Censor Certificate

Universal

Statutory Warning from Mukesh

If you're worried that the book will contain a lot of information on Telugu cinema and culture, you're right. If you think this book isn't for you because you don't know anything about the subject, then you're wrong.

PS: Smoking and drinking are injurious to health.

Title Card

The Age of Heroes

Primary Cast Introduction

Nandamuri Taraka Rama Rao (NTR): The first male superstar for the Telugu people, especially in the decades stretching from the '50s to the '70s. NTR launched his own party in the state, called the Telugu Desam Party (TDP), and became chief minister of the state. **Chiranjeevi:** The unchallenged male superstar of the '80s and '90s. He, too, started his own political party, called the Praja Rajyam Party (PRP). It lasted only one election, and he failed to make the big political splash expected of him. He later merged the PRP with the Congress party. Now, he's back to acting in films.

Vijayashanthi: The most popular female lead. When on-screen, Vijayashanthi played a diverse range of roles and, in the second half of her career, she played characters that were morally right and incorruptible. She danced, she titillated audience, but, more importantly, she terrified villains — male villains. She has been a politician and has had careers in multiple parties, including the Bharatiya Janata Party (BJP), the Congress, the Bharat Rashtra Samithi (formerly known as the Telangana Rashtra Samithi or TRS). She was briefly at the helm of her own Talli Telangana Party.

Pawan Kalyan: Chiranjeevi's younger brother, who was also a superstar, but mostly popular with the young male population of the

Telugu states. Started his own political party called the Jana Sena Party (JSP). The JSP won one seat in the 2019 Andhra Pradesh state elections. It wasn't Chiranjeevi. He lost in both the constituencies from where he fought. He has now re-entered cinema, while running the party.

R. Narayana Murthy: Actor popular in the '80s and '90s for acting in Red cinema, which glorified protests and protest culture, the Left parties, the Naxalite movement. He himself has never been a political candidate for any party.

Supporting Actors

Telugu Audience: Made of nearly 8.5 crore people. They were once part of a unified Telugu state called Andhra Pradesh. In 2014, this audience was split across two states – Telangana and Andhra Pradesh. The Telugu audience is usually squabbling over caste, their favourite heroes, food and the state of the Telugu language.

Hero Introduction Shot

There are Pied Pipers waiting for us. They lure us out of our homes, and we follow them in swarms where we shed our money for them. We visit them with our families, with our friends and sometimes in dark corners with our romantic partners. Once seated, these Pied Pipers drag us out of our seats and lift us into a world whose grammar is flexible – much like their bodies. They dance, sing, beat people to pulp … they will defend the right and punish the wrong, they will show us the monuments of the world, they are willing to do anything to make people follow them. In their hands, the story-writing commandment of 'the world changes the character' is inverted and becomes 'the character changes the world'.

These Pied Pipers, like the smell of ripe mangoes in the kitchen, waft into conversations with families in our homes. They seep into our fantasies once the lights are turned off. They sometimes exaggerate our flaws as well as society's, like distorted mirrors do; at other times, like convex mirrors, they bloat our egos. They muddy our reality and make us glad it happened.

But there are many in this country who can do that trick. Bollywood has produced countless Kapoors, Khannas, Khans and Kumars who've made the nation dance to their tune.

But the Pied Pipers of Telugu cinema are different – because they want to pull one more trick, which separates the tricksters from the magicians. They are not satisfied that we paid money to watch their act and listen to their tune; they want us to pay with something more important than money – votes. When they plunder our political will at the ballot box, that's when you know that they are the aiming for greatness. They will use every weapon they have – including their region, religion, caste, gender, their fathers and grandfathers. Some are successful, most come close.

These Pied Pipers in the Telugu states are called *Heroes*.

Song and Dance

The Telugu film industry, which produces the greatest number of films in the country, has a fascinating obsession with its masculine protagonists. While most begin as 'actors' playing a part in the broader story, as success beckons, the scripts begin to bend around these Heroes. This phenomenon is not the result of individual egos, but a cultural phenomenon that defines the state of the Telugu society today, and explores the cultural vacuum that Heroes, the 'mass' stars of the Telugu film industry, occupy and dictate.

Comedy Track and First Fight in a Strange Land

As with all catastrophes, the idea for this book struck me when I decided to tell the truth.

I was new to Mumbai and barely knew anybody in the city. In the process of making friends, I piled on to colleagues, friends of friends, acquaintances ... and all this usually meant socializing with strangers, while feigning curiosity in activities in which I had no palpable interest. Loud concerts, eating undercooked dinners prepared by new friends and lying about its quality over the fear of losing a nascent friendship, watching experimental theatre where actors poured paint over each other to encourage thespian ambitions of friends of friends. In this process, questions would be asked of my work, my interests and, more importantly, where I was from. And I would always lie to these strangers who had the potential to be best friends – *Hyderabad.*

People would nod and usually tell me about the last time they were in the city. Some would extend a friendly arm by telling me how much they loved the biriyani from the city. I would lie about how my opinion concurred with theirs. Some would try to be cheeky and goad me by telling me that they preferred biriyani from other cities. I would pretend with equal cheekiness about how offended I was.

'Facts don't care about your opinions,' I would say. Or if I was really trying to fit in and extract laughs out of the conversation, I would say: 'The Nizams loved the biriyani so much, they didn't conquer further south. My biriyani stopped wars. What did yours do?'

It would get the laughs. I would make a friend for the evening.

But if I were being honest, I would have said: *I don't care about biriyani. More importantly, I'm not from Hyderabad.*

I continued hiding the truth – partly out of embarrassment.

Partly.

Until the day that I almost made a friend. Let's call him Amit. He mentioned that the spelling of his name doesn't end with an H. He accused South Indians of squeezing the alphabet into a name even when not required. I replied that I didn't foresee a situation where I had to write his name down, but I thanked him for the information. Then he asked me where I was from, and I almost gave him the same answer I would always give. But this time around, I wanted to tell him the truth. I marvelled at Amit's confidence as he ensured that I knew the correct spelling of his name, while I brushed over an important aspect of my life like it was a bald spot on the head. With a false sense of confidence, I told him the truth.

Anantapur.

Then Amit's face froze – his brows furrowed while his brain tried to locate the place like a navigation system running on low battery. It scanned the map of the country – first checking around the foothills of the Himalayas; then dusting the Thar Desert, hoping it would be released; groping along the long coast of India, going all the way from Mumbai to Kolkata. For a brief second, he even glanced at the seven states in the northeast. Finally, he gave up what seemed like a futile search and reached into the interiors of India, like a magician looking for a rabbit that may have escaped from the hat. From the Ganga, he combed through till he reached the Narmada, his fingers caressing the Deccan Plateau like it was a big mole on clear skin, until he reached Kanyakumari. He peeked into the Andaman and Nicobar Islands, knowing full well that this would not be successful.

I wanted to help him.

'It's in Andhra Pradesh,' I finally said. Without pausing for a second, Amit said: 'Andhra Pradesh? I once took a train that went through Andhra Pradesh.'

Villain Is Introduced

Amit was only the final domino in this quest. It had taken years to come here. Maybe it began when I was reading my first 'Indian' book by a celebrated male Indian author – the kind who gets to roam with Hollywood stars and starlets – talk about Indian-ness by talking about Bollywood as Indian cinema. Or maybe it was in the way small towns were spoken about in Indian literature – emerging through streets in Uttar Pradesh, posters on walls in Bihar, quirky villagers in Tamil Nadu.

Maybe it had to do with names. Indian English literature had a standardized way of writing names: First Name – Last Name. Characters and their creators had stylized names in this fashion. But how could I make peace with this tradition? Where I come from, this tradition is flipped. Surname first and then the 'first' name. That's how Telugu names are intended to be read, and to me, the 'normal' way feels as if one is being coerced into a headstand, talking to people's feet and listening through their toes.

It could also be that Indian books that spoke about India harped on about India's cities – about Mumbai's maximum nature, its lanes and rum-soaked bars; Delhi and how each alley had a history, and any historian worth their salt fought over the origin of each brick and bridge in the city; Kolkata with its intellectuals; Lucknow with its poets, and Bangalore with its laid-back character like a beer-guzzling friend, who enjoys coding on breezy Sunday evenings. *But what about the small streets? What about the gullies of Anantapur? Or any of the hundred small towns in the Telugu states?*

Even if one looks at the map of India for long enough, it is still easy to miss these places, for there is nothing terrifyingly remarkable about them. They don't have the metaphysical allure of the Himalayas or the expansive coastline of the Peninsula or the mystique of the northeast or the devouring fervour of a city from the Third World. They can't even boast of the kingdoms and royalty that the Thar desert has to offer. Somewhere in the south-central region of Peninsular India, these places exist as trains and highways cut across them – as if God had doodled during a boring lecture.

Heroes are useful to understand these towns and its people, who are otherwise so easy to ignore. They are all unified in how much they worship their Heroes. They might not even be devotees to the same gods, but when a Hero walks on-screen, there's unity. For two-and-a-half hours, at least.

Key Death and the Interval Twist

There isn't much conversation to have when there's a dead body in front of you. That was another moment that spurred me on to write a book on what Telugu Heroes can do.

My grandmother lay in an icebox, while my family and I surrounded it and mourned. Uncles and aunts took care of the rituals and the red tape that come with Hindu death ceremonies. The smoke from the incense sticks, like a ballet dancer with wings, floated towards the skies along with my grandmother's soul and her love for Telugu films. She probably wanted to have watched one more film. And not on television – no – but in a darkened theatre, where the old sponge seats are dusty, the floor smells of cheap phenyl, and the auditorium is crammed with people like the sweets in the jar in her kitchen. But here she was – dead and unsatisfied.

This was the first *real* death I had ever encountered.

There were faint grumbles about rituals not being performed to perfection, the tea that was being served not being hot enough, some people saying they needed to leave soon as they had planes to catch. I stood a little away, staring at the space between the front wheels and back wheels of the ice box. Had I looked any higher, I would see the pale body that once had ripe-sapodilla-coloured skin and was full of life. The moment seemed endless until, a young cousin – no more than twelve years old, with a faint moustache and skin the colour of fresh ginger tea – walked up to me and said, 'Do you want to go for a Mahesh Babu film after this? I'm bored.'

~Intermission~

Flashback with Heroine

I must make a confession. My obsession with Telugu cinema and its Heroes began after falling in love with a woman. I was six years old, and she was my English teacher – Fathima Miss. She would walk into class every day and remove her black burqa. When she walked in, the air smelled better; when she smiled, schoolbags became lighter than clouds; and when she spoke in perfect English, it made young hearts skip beats, like a flat stone skimming on water.

Every time she walked in during the English period, we would turn into Romeos; and when we looked up at her, we felt what the doomed Shakespearean hero must have felt standing underneath Juliet's balcony.

I counted myself lucky when I discovered that Fathima Miss was unmarried, because on the off chance that she accepted my proposal, there was at least one less hurdle to cross on our quest to becoming lovers. I had imagined a beautiful future for Fathima Miss and me, in which we overcame religion and age differences to get married. She would be the only breadwinner of our family till I came of age. We would come to school together, as husband and wife, as student and teacher, swatting away society's scornful gaze. I was sure I could make the relationship work, but first, I had to convince Fathima Miss that I could be the man of her dreams. I tried many tricks that I devoured from Telugu films, beginning with a love letter that went like this:

I love you, Miss. You will marry me?

Thankfully, I threw away the letter because I lacked the requisite courage to hand it over. I then tried giving her a rose and a balloon, like I had seen in a film, but my plans were pricked when I couldn't justify at home why I needed those two objects. It continued like this, when an opportunity one day appeared out of thin air, like gods appeared in black-and-white films. This time again, a Hero came to my rescue.

In one class, attempting to break our boredom, she asked us to talk in English about our favourite Telugu Heroes. She began by confessing that her favourite was Pawan Kalyan – then a young actor. All the boys copied her answer, hoping that common interests would lead to a future with Fathima Miss. She assumed it was a coincidence; such was the angelic innocence of Fathima Miss. But I wondered what about Pawan Kalyan impressed her. I assumed that maybe if I imitated him and filled in the gap between him and me, I could achieve my dreamy future with her. I forced my family to take me to a film that featured Pawan Kalyan. In the film, he played a wastrel younger brother who would go on to become a boxer to avenge his elder brother, whose career was cut short by an unscrupulous villain.

It became evident that I didn't have the build to be a boxer.

But in the film, he does something superhuman that I decided to copy. He, with no help from computer-generated effects, manages to have over ten cars drive over his bare knuckles. It was a real stunt that shook the Telugu people as nobody before him had performed such extreme feats for the sake of entertaining an audience. They were wowed by this young actor, who carried the legacy of his elder brother, but was desperate to break away from nepotistic shackles. He captured the imagination of the state – and at least one English teacher tucked away in a small town had lost her heart to this stunt. Or so I was convinced. And if having cars run over my knuckles was what it took to impress Fathima Miss, then that's what I would do.

I found the perfect street. It had been freshly laid with black tar and cars had begun to take this road. There was also a hospital down the road which meant that in case I had to be rushed there then the same car that once stood on my knuckles could drive me to the emergency ward. I had also chosen a street as far humanly possible as I could walk, so that I could avoid family members. I congratulated myself for my well-rounded mature thinking.

The plan was simple. I would lie prostrate on the ground, and hopefully, a car would run over my upturned palms. On a hot Sunday, and on a hotter road, I lay prostrate on the ground to impress the woman of my dreams. If I could be like her favourite Hero, then we could get the happy ending I dreamt for the both of us.

Except, I wasn't a Hero and real life wasn't a Telugu film.

I was scolded by a passer-by and those that recognized me as the boy who lived a few streets down the road rightly took me to my parents. The faces of my parents turned hotter than the black tar road. They took turns hitting me, like a TV remote that refused to work.

Later that year, Fathima Miss would get married and move away to a faraway town. Neither Pawan Kalyan nor I would get our 'happily ever after' with Fathima Miss. But there were multiple scars that were left behind because of her, not least the wounds from the thrashing I got from my parents. There developed in me a deep-seated need to impress English teachers but, more importantly, a childhood fascination with Telugu Heroes.

While I lived my life like an ordinary human, they could do superhuman feats like have cars run over their knuckles and win the heart of Fathima Miss.

Montage Song

Let's avoid the term 'regional' cinema. Refer to it as Telugu cinema, Tamil cinema, Kannada cinema, Malayalam cinema or Tulu cinema.

Protagonist Becomes Hero of the People

All Indian film industries have produced stars, megastars and superstars. But one peculiarity differentiates the Telugu film industry from others: Telugu films don't just produce stars, they manufacture 'Heroes'.

In the 'mass' films in which these Heroes predominantly act, they are shown performing outstanding acts of courage, as sources of moral guidance, creating prototypes for a man in the modern era. Therefore, films in the Telugu-speaking states not only imitate life, but they set a template for it – a blueprint and guide to approach life.

These mass stars are elevated to such a high status that after conquering the popular Telugu imagination, a leap into the political sphere is not just the logical next step, it is almost inevitable. Some, like NTR, are extremely successful; some, like Chiranjeevi, end up as spectacular disasters; and some, like Pawan Kalyan, end up with a mixed bag of experiences, chugging towards a hopeful political future.

These Heroes are not aberrations to the way of life in the Telugu-speaking states, but a result of the current sociocultural space. *The Age of Heroes* will explore the reasons behind the rise of the 'Telugu Hero' – not actor, not star, but Hero with a capital H.

Mandatory Item Song

I am not sure if you know everything you need to know to fully understand Telugu Cinema and its obsession with Heroes. I don't think anybody really does. But when you're in a darkened auditorium, with hundreds of other people, before the title card comes, there's an invisible contract being signed by everyone present:

> Look I understand none of this stuff is real. But it's so much fun when it happens. This is not mere escapism; it's an addiction. This is a mass drug that we are all consuming. Once I leave, I may discuss and dissect it, think I'm superior to it, inferior to it, model my life around it, vote for the Hero when they become a politician, but, in this auditorium, I am an addict.
>
> Signed By
[Name of Audience]

Hero's Final Warning to the Villain

The first chapter of this book will delve into the power of the folk tales, myth and divinity that has seeped into the Telugu consciousness. All mainstream Telugu films are folk tales. Not just the actions of these heroes, even the themes and tropes in these films stem from and are steeped in folk traditions.

In the second chapter, the book analyses the failure of the Telugu society to spread the culture of reading across social barriers and hierarchies. It locates the culture of reading and writing across centuries, arguing that the reason folk tales have survived is because of the decay in reading habits and writing culture in the state.

From locating the Hero with factors 'outside' of cinema, the journey moves inwards as the third chapter is dedicated to understanding the way caste shapes the creation of these Heroes and the rearrangement of social capital that occurs due to the mere existence of Heroes. To understand the cast, it uses one genre, 'Red Cinema', peculiar to Telugu Cinema, and one star who belonged to the genre.

The fourth chapter explores the uniqueness of the Telugu 'fan'. It argues that Heroes are made by the devotion shown by their fans. The chapter uses the lens of masculinity, mentorship and the vacuum of political icons plaguing the state to explore what makes a fan devote their time to a Hero.

And finally, the book ends by using as a case study a female Hero, Vijayashanthi, known for her iconic 'angry', anti-establishment roles, which are usually reserved for men.

Twist in the Climax and the Real Villain

One final confession before the book begins.

Part of the reason I needed to write this book was because I found myself being a bully. A young teenage cousin confided in me about how he had found an artist whose music deeply resonated with him. The lyrics helped him lighten the load of the world off his thirteen-year-old shoulders. His endearing earnestness should have made me gentle in how I spoke to him. Instead, I shamed him for his taste in music and humiliated him – a punishment for confiding in me. I saw him take a leap of faith and plunge into an abyss of disgrace. To date, the soured relationship continues to worsen.

It was upsetting, because not only did I lose a precious ally in the family but also, unknown to me, I had travelled to the diametrically opposite end in the circle of shame. When I was as old as him, I too felt apprehensive in admitting that I loved Telugu cinema, hiding my interest like a child hiding a cough in front of a doctor with syringes. It came from the assumption that if I found meaning in Telugu cinema and culture, then I would be tied down to only this cinema and culture – especially at a time when Telugu cinema protagonists were comically defying physics on-screen. Vulgarity, regressive attitudes and dialogues, and nonsensical screenplays mutated my shame into deep contempt.

My family, too, encouraged me to shave away any love for Telugu cinema in the hope that it would give me a more modernized and Westernized outlook to life. At least watching English films can teach me the language, while Telugu films only taught me that with the right background music, a punch from the Hero armed with a dialogue could change society. Despite enjoying this cinema, my own family shamed themselves for their film habits and culture. It was *bad* culture, and they wanted their child to escape.

End Card

The film is over. The lights come on. The Hero has changed the world and his world lives happily ever after. You go back home. The effect of the drug will eventually wear off, but the drug will remain inside.

The Pied Piper story is supposed to have two different types of endings: The one in which the children live happily ever after on top of a mountain; and the other, where the children are led off a cliff. Telugu Heroes, too, take the Telugu people on a journey with all kinds of endings – making the audience dance to their tunes, enticing them as voters to the ballot boxes, and leading them to countless mountain tops and off cliffs.

This is the story of that journey.

2

Anaganaga: Once Upon a Time

'While he was alive, he was impossible to ignore; once he had gone, he was impossible to imitate.'

– Shashi Tharoor, *The Great Indian Novel*

When the Hero Enters

My grandmother was a teller of terrible bedtime stories. As a young boy, lying next to her on the terrace – where clothes were hung out to dry – I'd inadvertently ask her to tell me a story before going to sleep. Most nights were comfortable – starry black skies, soft quilts stitched from her old sarees, cool uninterrupted breeze. But when she broke into a story, the night's belly was cut open to terrors. Each one began the same way: '*Anaganaga ...* Once upon a time.' But they all had their own macabre ending.

Once upon a time there was a young boy who was travelling in a bus. It was nighttime, and he was asleep. He hadn't had dinner because he wanted to sleep more. Bad boy. Other people were also asleep. Suddenly, at around 11, the bus crashed into another one. Both busses caught fire. In the chaos, the boy woke up. He tried to help the other passengers. Even though he did his best, he couldn't save all of them. Later, his parents came and took him back home. He had dinner and slept.

'What happened next?' I would ask her.

'What happens after you sleep? You have dreams,' she would reply.

'What is that sound?' I would ask, hoping that she would redeem herself if I gave her creative fodder for a second story.

'That's the sound of Lord Brahma on his vehicle, coming to look for children who aren't asleep.'

'What happens to children who aren't asleep?'

'He takes them away.'

Horrified, I'd shut my eyes. Hoping for the sound to not come any closer, I would plunge into a panic-induced sleep. Later, I was relieved to find that the sound of Brahma's vehicle was actually the chirping of crickets, and no children had ever been abducted.

My grandmother made up for her lack of creativity in stories through the complete power she had over one object in the house – the television remote. Like a country with imperialist ambitions, she would barge into the living room and the remote would gravitate towards her arthritic palms. Perhaps my parents gave it to her, but to me, it seemed to appear magically in her hands, like the cheap graphics in the mythological soaps that she loved to watch. One day, my father was flipping through channels to find news about the changing political tides in Andhra Pradesh, when the likes of Bill Gates and Bill Clinton were sharing the dais with the state's then chief minister, N. Chandrababu Naidu. They were exciting times in my father's life. To see one of 'us' share the stage with one of the world's richest and most powerful was a proud moment for him, almost as if a man was sharing the stage with gods. In his quest, my father paused briefly on ETV Telugu, which was playing *Pathala Bhairavi* – the first Telugu blockbuster and a folklore film. Much like the goddess in the film, my grandmother appeared out of nowhere and demanded that the film be played, because it featured her favourite actor – Nandamuri Taraka Rama Rao (NTR). My father was a stern man and seeing him turned into an obedient son was a refreshing change. I presume he told himself that photos in the newspaper next day would have to do.

On that hot Andhra afternoon towards the end of summer, when it felt as if the sun hadn't been told that its season had passed, my grandmother introduced me to the world of *Pathala Bhairavi*.

Once upon a time, there was a brave young man who worked as a gardener in the palace of the king of Ujjayani. His name was Ramudu, but everyone called him Thota Ramudu, 'Ramudu who works in the garden'. Upon seeing the princess of the land, Indumati, Thota Ramudu fell in love with her beauty and her childlike earnestness. Under the moonlit skies, she seemed like another moon to him. Indumati, reluctant at first, began to reciprocate Ramudu's feelings, taken by his charm and bravery, despite his status as a commoner. Once, Thota Ramudu saved her from a poisonous cobra, but unlike most people, he didn't beat it with a stick. He picked it up with his bare hands and flung it far away from Indumati. On another occasion, Thota Ramudu managed to humiliate Indumati's pesky and dim-witted uncle, Surasena, who wanted to marry her at any cost. The king of the land did not approve of this alliance, especially after learning from the royal priests that due to a fault in her stars, a grave evil was headed Indumati's way, and she would need a strong and brave person to protect her.

The evil headed towards the princess was an evil sorcerer known as Nepala Mantrikudu, 'The Sorcerer from Nepal'. He lived in the mountains near Ujjayani and had discovered a way to unleash the powers of Pathala Bhairavi, the goddess of the underworld, by either sacrificing a sorcerer like himself or a young man whose bravery had no match. If Nepala Mantrikudu succeeded, then he would need only say, 'Jai Pathala Bhairavi' and the goddess would grant him any boon he wished for.

Nepala Mantrikudu already had magical powers hidden in his long and ugly beard, but he wanted more. So he went looking for a brave man and came upon Thota Ramudu climbing the walls of the palace secretly in the middle of the night to reach the chambers of the princess. Concluding that this young man must be the bravest, Nepala Mantrikudu set out to Ujjayani, along with his assistant, Sajadapa, to lure the young man into his caves.

Surasena caught Thota Ramudu in the princess' chambers and convinced the king to throw Ramudu into the dungeons before hanging him publicly. However, the king was a gentle patriarch and respected the wishes of his daughter. He told Ramudu that he could wed Indumati, but on one condition – that he must amass wealth worthy of a princess. Determined, Thota Ramudu set out to gain wealth at any cost. But driven by passion, Ramudu ended up falling into the trap laid by Nepala Mantrikudu. The sorcererled him into the underworld, full of horrors unheard of – spinning blades of sharp rock that could chop up mountains, fiery coals that could tear a hole through the earth they are on, and horrors that could shake the fiercest warrior to his core. With the help of divine intervention and sheer bravery, Ramudu reached the depths of the netherworld to Pathala Bhairavi with Nepala Mantrikudu following him in close pursuit. Using his spontaneity, Thota Ramudu managed to outwit Nepala Mantrikudu and sacrificed him, thus obtaining the powers of the goddess stored in a statue. Then Thota Ramudu asked, 'Jai Pathala Bhairavi.' She appeared and said, 'Oh, human, what is your wish?' In the end, Ramudu returned with the magical statue, a palace, abundant wealth – becoming worthy of Indumati.

But the story does not end happily.

Using dark magic, Sajadapa managed to restore Nepala Mantrikudu, who now wanted revenge on Thota Ramudu. On the day Ramudu and Indumati were to wed, using the rejected and dejected Surasena, Nepala Mantrikudu managed to steal the statue. All of Thota Ramudu's wealth disappeared in a flash. Worse still, under Surasena's watch, Nepala Mantrikudu kidnapped Indumati, away from her kingdom and into the caves that were his hiding place.

Later, filled with remorse, Surasena confessed the truth to Thota Ramudu and asked him to save Indumati. Like a man looking for a needle amongst a million needles, Thota Ramudu, along with his friend Anji, set out to look for the lair of the evil sorcerer.

Meanwhile, in captivity, Indumati was livid. She rebuked Nepala Mantrikudu, telling him to fight like a man. 'Defeat Thota Ramudu instead of coercing me into marriage,' she told him. Nepala Mantrikudu was outraged hearing these words. Using the powers of Pathala Bhairavi, he summoned Ramudu to the caves and tied him up. Now left alone, Anji chanced upon some magical beings in the forest, and managed to get his hands on an invisible cloak and shoes that can make one float. He reached the dungeons where Ramudu was being held captive, released him, and gave him the cloak and shoes. Anji then dressed up as Sajadapa and convinced Nepala Mantrikudu to shave his magical beard, so that he could appear as handsome as Thota Ramudu to Indumati. Vain and vengeful, Nepala Mantrikudu agreed. In doing so, he lost his powers, confident that the statue he possessed would be sufficient for his evil plans. He then proceeded to Indumati's chambers to impress her with his new look. But once there, he realized that Thota Ramudu had taken her place. The enraged sorcerer attacked Anji and Thota Ramudu, and a duel ensured. Anji managed to steal the statue, while Thota Ramudu fought off Nepala Mantrikudu, finally killing him.

The ordeal over, Indumati, Anji and Thota Ramudu returned safely to the kingdom of Ujjayani – along with the wealth that had disappeared and the statue of Pathala Bhairavi. Before the kingdom could carry on with their happily ever after, they decided to ask Pathala Bhairavi for one final boon – that not only the people of Ujjayani, but also those who have heard or seen the story shall live happily ever after.

Jai Pathala Bhairavi.

At the end of the film, my grandmother let out a short 'Jai Pathala Bhairavi' with an excited clap of her hands. She vividly recalled watching the film when it released in theatres in 1951, and being completely mesmerized by it – its world, its myth, the words the film invented. Even the villain was beloved by everyone; she remembered conversations loaded with references to the way he twisted Telugu words. She remembered being excited by the visual effects of the film, which felt so real – the floating palace towards the end of the film felt real; the garden under the moonlit nights felt real; and when the villain walked through a door, it felt real. She laughed at the naivety of all the people in the auditorium, but she justified it by telling me that people in towns in Tamil Nadu tried to touch the waters when Thota Ramudu walked past a beach. I had little faith in my grandmother ability to be unbiased. But she insisted that's the truth.

The First Hero

When Telugu audiences watch films, they don't like the bitter taste of Heroes dying. Those sorts of tragedies aren't why cinema goers love the medium. The villain can kill everybody and anybody around the Hero, the villain can torture the Hero in countless ways, but the fun is in knowing that the Hero will defeat the villain. Everyone knows the end, but it's about how the Hero gets there – or rather, the one who gets there becomes the Hero. The Hero doesn't survive because he's the Hero; he is a Hero because he survives. When people watched Thota Ramudu's story, it was obvious this guy was a winner. But how does he get there? What strange lands does he visit? What does he concoct in the face of adversity? These are the questions the film tries to answer. Thota Ramudu was the first folk Hero on-screen who changed what the Telugu audience expected from their cinema. Mainstream cinema at the time told stories of already deified figures, such as the saint-poet Vemana, or sermonizing social dramas such as *Jeevitham* (Life). Protagonists in such cinema showed exemplary ways of living, spoke to the people from behind the silver screen – none truly spoke like the people whom it was meant to entertain. There were no protagonists who emerged from the mass imagination.

Then came Thota Ramudu – an action hero who defeated the evil villain, but he did it with swagger and uncombed hair. He could climb the palace walls, he could charm and meet the princess in the dead of the night, he could make the king's brother-in-law look like a buffoon, and he could make the punishment of getting hanged the next day feel like an experience the audience was missing out on. He represented angry workers toiling away underneath Zamindars, a man who was tired of hearing about his place in the system. Thota Ramudu told the world that being born a gardener didn't mean they had to die as one. The film gave him a mantra, an adapted version of 'fortune favours the brave' – *Dhairye sahase Lakshmi*. If one fought hard enough and bravely rebelled against the system, they need not live under the rule of others.

The people of Ujjayani have two peculiar alternate names for Thota Ramudu. One is *Bhale* Ramudu, where 'bhale' loosely translates to 'Hail' or 'Superb' and is an exclamation reserved for praise following a Heroic deed. The other, more interesting name is the word '*Kathanayakudu*' – meaning Hero. In an early scene, when there are dancers and musicians entertaining the villagers, the travelling troupe asks if there are any brave men amongst them and everyone turns to Thota Ramudu. He awkwardly steers the looks away from him, indicating that he is uncomfortable with the attention. But the song and dance are disrupted by Surasena, who argues that entertainment is dangerous and begins to collect a tax that he has cooked up on the spot. Suddenly, Thota Ramudu jumps into action and thrashes Surasena and his soldiers – not caring for Surasena's royal lineage. With this one act of bravado, Ramudu instils courage into the hearts of the common people. Thota Ramudu, the hero, the *kathanayakudu*, saves the people of Ujjayani.

The song that was being sung by the dance troupe was about how the lesson to learn from history is that at the turn of every age, a Hero shall rise and lead its people to freedom and prosperous times. Once Surasena runs away fearing for his life, all the people of Ujjayani chant '*Kathanayakudu ki Jai* (Hail the Hero)'. This direct reference to the protagonist is jarring, but clarifies what the expectations from him are – to usher in the promised good tidings for the era. Later in the film, when Anji notices Thota Ramudu express sadness, on the brink of tears, because the love of his life is missing and could be anywhere within the ambit of the known world, he reminds Thota Ramudu that he is a Hero, and a Hero doesn't cry. *Mustn't* cry. He calls him just that – neither Thota Ramudu nor Bhale Ramudu, but *kathanayakudu*, Hero.

The villain of the film, Nepala Mantrikudu, was a clear outsider, threatening the peaceful kingdom. He could conjure up any magic, but his Telugu was so silly that it was tough to not laugh at him. The terrifying villain was made toothless by his awkward pronunciation of words beginning with 'cha', which he pronounced as 'sya'. It's like a speed breaker to the menace that Samarla Venkata Ranga Rao (popularly known as S.V. Ranga Rao), who plays Nepala Mantrikudu, brings to the character. He intersperses his dialogue with Hindi words like 'pasand' and other non-local words like 'bulbul', and uses made up words like 'dingri' and 'dimbhaka' confidently. His assistant is called Sajadapa, a random arrangement of consonants – like an untrained singer trying to move their mouth around the basics of Indian classical music. It was like K.V. Reddy, the director, and writer, Pingali Nagendra Rao, were saying, 'These outsiders have power with them, and we don't have much to begin with, but how tough can they be if they can't pronounce words a five-year-old can.' So *Pathala Bhairavi* gave the starved audience a Telugu folk Hero to devour, and an outsider who, despite the peril he brings with him, was laughable.

This is barely a coincidence, because post-Independence Andhra Pradesh was a strange place. It wasn't even Andhra Pradesh. The Telugu-speaking regions were split across geopolitical blobs called Madras Presidency, with an administrative capital set up in Madras and Hyderabad, then ruled by the Nizams. Freedom had been won from the British, but in the aftermath, Madras was an uneasy place for the Telugu people, for whom two key developments were taking place.

The first was the growing demand for a separate state. Then Chief Minister Tanguturi Prakasam Pantulu had managed to broker a soft peace under the nationalist freedom movement. Leaders would work together till the departure of the British and then resume the discussion on the fate of the Telugu people. Since the early twentieth century, there was a growing feeling of regional pride and the notion that because of the overpowering voice of Tamil leaders in the Dravidian movement, Telugu voices were getting subdued. The tension made itself apparent after Independence, and Madras (now Chennai) became a battleground for space. Through the Madras Manadhe (Madras is Ours) movement, Telugu leaders called for the integration of Madras into the Telugu-speaking regions. Tamil leaders quoted the Tamil epic *Silappathikaram* (The Tale of the Anklet), where the northern borders of the kingdom include the temple town of Tirupati and Madras.

The other key development in these regions was the influx of Leftist literature and the influence of Leftist thinkers – into the Telugu-speaking regions in both Madras and Hyderabad. Marxist literature was smuggled in, translated and circulated by the early Leftist groups as pamphlets and through underground magazines, including the works of thinkers such as Maxim Gorky. With the early withdrawal of the Civil Disobedience Movement, frustrated youth found solace in Leftist writings and ideology. Organizations such as the Peasant Protection League were formed by intellectuals to educate people on their rights. Leaders like Garimella Satyanarayana injected ideology into folk songs without literary baggage, which sat easier on tongues. The Indian People's Theatre Association (IPTA) set up regional branches – the one in Andhra being known as *Praja Natya Mandali* (People's Theatre Congregation), which gave folk singers, dancers and storytellers an official platform, while retaining their flavour. Regional oral storytelling folk forms such as Burra

Katha (meaning tambourine story, which consisted of folk tales) and Hari Katha (meaning stories of god), gained popularity in Telangana and Andhra. Oral storytellers would often travel across towns in Andhra Pradesh, particularly during festivals such as Sankranti and Ugadi. Over time, folk stories seeped into the popular imagination, aided by Leftist thought and an enthusiasm for the revival of local art forms.

Meanwhile, late in 1952, about a year and a half after the release of *Pathala Bhairavi*, the agitation for a separate state took a more incendiary turn – with prominent Gandhian Potti Sreeramulugoing on a fast unto death. Ramulu had taken up the cause of Dalits being allowed entry into temples in his hometown of Nellore, the southern coastal town of Andhra Pradesh. He had given up a cushy job in the Railways to learn from Gandhi in Sabarmati Ashram. In 1952, fed up with the government, which had reached a stalemate over the fate of Madras, Potti Sreeramulu went on a fast, demanding for a separate statehood for the Telugu states. That the fast was held in Madras – the very place that was up for contention – made the event iconic. Tamil leaders were adamant to not let go of either Madras or Tirupati. Jawaharlal Nehru tried to placate Sreeramulu, but because there was no official agreement on statehood, it only made the latter more resolute.

Perhaps nobody really expected Potti Sreeramulu to carry on with the fast until the bitter end. It had only happened once before – by Jatin Das, in a prison in Lahore, under British rule. Surely nobody would do it against'our own', people would have thought. In most cases of fast-unto-death, the leadership usually intervened with an offer that would get the person to break their fast. But with Sreeramulu, it seemed impossible to reach an agreement, even as days became weeks. Jawaharlal Nehru, Vallabhbhai Patel and Pattabi Sitharamayya formed the JVP committee, borrowing the first letter from each of their names. Under it, they came up with many creative solutions: splitting Madras into two parts along the Cooum River; distributing the city to the states; making it a joint capital; making Madras a centrally administered region. But Telugu leaders continued to insist on 'Madras Manadhe', while Tamil leaders argued that Madras and Tirupati were theirs.

After fifty-eight days of fasting, in the early hours of 16 December 1952, Potti Sreeramulu passed away, becoming the first person in history of Independent India to die because of a fast unto death, in a crusade against the government. A non-violent protest ended in violence as riots erupted in parts of Andhra. In January 1953, sensing that the issue was getting out of hand, the government announced a new state of Andhra Pradesh for the Telugu-speaking people. Madras wouldn't be part of the state, but Tirupati would belong to the Telugu people. An uneasy peace was brokered, with a temporary capital set in the historical town of Kurnool.

It wasn't the ideal situation for the Telugu people, but it sufficed at the time. Potti Sreeramulu became the first Hero for the Telugu people, who fought against outsiders to bring good tidings for his people. He was posthumously conferred with the title of 'Amarajeevi' ('Immortal Being' or one who never dies).

Like I said, Telugu people don't like it when their Heroes die.

Curly Hair Over Vowels

There are many things that *Pathala Bhairavi* and its creators got right. First is flattening out the internal contradictions within the story and framework they chose. The villain is an outsider, yes, but the entire setting is foreign to the Telugu audience. The story is set in Ujjain, a kingdom in Rajasthan, with no relation to Telugu people. An important way of overcoming this hurdle was to play on the way Telugu language digests foreign words.

There's a scene in the Tamil comedy film *Panchatanthiram*, starring Kamal Hassan, Simran and Ramya Krishnan that comedically captures the essence of what Telugu does. A comedy of errors leads a traditional Telugu joint family to believe that Maggie, the 'call girl', is the wife of Ram, the protagonist, and they begin to treat her like they would treat his real wife. This angers Ram's real wife, the Tamilian Mythili, who accuses the Telugu family of being in the 'call girl' business. When the ageing patriarch doesn't understand the word 'business', she translates the word for him thus: 'business-u'. He then understands the meaning immediately.

Telugu is unique in that all words end with vowels. It gives the language an inherently musical tonality, but it is also a distinct marker of a word being absorbed by Telugu speakers. The language has nearly eighteen distinct vowel sounds, which makes the process easier. It's a way of stamping words with originality, while giving the language the space to evolve. Words borrowed from other languages take on this quality: *jawaab* (answer) becomes *jawaabu* and *shikaar* (trip/hunt) become *shikaaru*; rail become *railu* (pronounced rye-lu) and nurse becomes *nursu*. Even gods are not spared: the Sanskrit 'Rama' becomes 'Ramudu'; 'Shiva' becomes 'Shivudu'. Similarly, in the film, Ujjain is renamed Ujjayani, suiting the Telugu palette and making it easier to believe that the place exists as an extension to Andhra Pradesh. Even the Rajasthani protagonist is called Ramudu and the princess' is named Indumati – with '*mati*' being what adds the Telugu flavour to the otherwise pan-Indian name 'Indu'.

Pathala Bhairavi borrows liberally from *Aladdin* as well as villains from Shakespeare's plays, adapting them and ensuring that it never alienates those seated in the theatres in small towns of Andhra Pradesh. The parallels to Aladdin's story are apparent in the premise of the princess and the commoner: the genie is substituted by the goddess Pathala Bhairavi; the evil vizier is portrayed by Nepala Mantrikudu; and – in a happy anachronistic coincidence – the monkey Abu from the 1992 Disney version is substituted with Anji (a short form for Anjaneyulu, the more common name in the Telugu states for Hanuman, the monkey god).

The Shakespearean touches are evident in the villain borrowing heavily from Shylock from *The Merchant of Venice* – in particular, his insecurities, his movements and his angst at being rejected by society. S.V. Ranga Rao, during his thespian years, was popular for playing Shylock on-stage. The makers also strike a fine balance in creating the perfect villain: hated for every second on-screen but loved forever once the audience leave the auditorium. Nepala Mantrikudu is undoubtedly the bad guy, a villain for the ages, but all his quirks made him a fan favourite. Once he loses the contest to the Hero, like a friend who tried to climb a mountain but failed during the last stretch, one wants to pat him on the back. In stage adaptations of the film, this character is often reserved for Telugu theatre's finest.

The most important element that the makers of *Pathala Bhairavi* got right was making efficient use of the lead actor, NTR, Telugu cinema's first Hero. NTR had acted as a protagonist in successful films before, but credit for those eluded him. In his first film, *Mana Desam* (Our Country), he played a small role as an inspector; in the film *Shavukaru* (Aristocrat), he played the protagonist but failed to become known for the role; the heroine of the film, *Janaki Sankramanchi*, rightfully stole all the adoration from the audience to such an extent that she rechristened herself with the film's title and became known as 'Shavukaru' Janaki.

In the film *Palletoori Pilla* (Village Belle), NTR played a goon who transforms because of the love of the heroine. Being the second hero to Akkineni Nageswara Rao (ANR) – by then a heartthrob and a bona-fide star – did not help. Besides, no heroism could match the vulnerability displayed by Anjali Devi's eyes as she played the titular village belle. Somehow, no film seemed to be using NTR's towering frame and his wild curly hair that seemed to protest against the softer characters he played.

In *Pathala Bhairavi*, NTR finally lets his hair loose without the teeth of a comb to tame it. He gets to fight bad guys, romance a princess in picturesque black-and-white settings under the moonlight, and even build a palace right opposite the king's palace. And ultimately, he manages to win over the princess and the love of the people of Ujjayani. He does all this while remaining a commoner.

Much of what I have to say of NTR and his charisma is sourced from my grandmother – there are few things in life that equal a grandmother describing the physical qualities of her favourite actor. She relished talking about his long curly hair – in Telugu, *ungarala juttu* (ring-shaped hair), – the brash walk in the palace gardens and, a little embarrassedly, she admits that she thought he sang the songs himself. For my grandmother, no star comes close to the young NTR walking under the moonlight in a garden, pining for his unattainable love. She even breaks into the song for me.

Kalavaramaaye madilo, naa madilo
Kalavaramaaye madilo, naa madilo
Kannulalona kalale aaye
Manase prema mandiramaaye
Kalavaramaaye madilo, naa madilo
Kalavaramaaye madilo, naa madilo

My mind has been disturbed,
My mind has been disturbed
My eyes have begun to dream
My heart has become abode of love
My mind has been disturbed,
My mind has been disturbed

At that point, she's not with me. She's back in a theatre in Guntur, the Andhra city that is known for chillies, pickles and tobacco.[1] Sneaking out of her house with her brothers under the pretext of going to the market, eating salted peanuts in theatres and enjoying a swashbuckling NTR chase after the princess in black-and-white in a stuffy, grimy theatre, as smoke from lit *beedis* kissed her cheeks and

---

1   Guntur is also where Helium was discovered by the scientist Jules Janssen.

rubbed the brown-coloured walls of the auditorium. My grandmother remembers singing this song for my grandfather. He was no NTR, but she remembers his hair before baldness crawled over his forehead till the back of his head – *ungarala juttu*. She argues that no stars from Tamil cinema, nobody from Hollywood, and not even the young Khans who follow their beloved from the cities in Europe to the mustard fields of Punjab, could match NTR being hopelessly in love.

Her obsession can be partly explained by the fact that her parents never told her stories. They couldn't afford school, and they left her with one book, *Pedda Bala Shiksha* – and nobody knew how it entered their house. An all-encompassing collection of moral stories, basic mathematics, games for children written in Telugu. It used to be a staple addition in Telugu houses, akin to Manorama yearbooks or Encyclopaedia Britannica. *Pedda Bala Shiksha* was for good boys and good girls who would grow up to be good adults, and according to my grandmother, it was for lazy parents who didn't know stories. She neither cared for the moral stories nor the differences between a square and rectangle, all explained in heavily Sanskritized Telugu.

Since she was part of the first few generations to experience cinema, the effect of the medium on her mind was truly sensational. She had seen puppet shows and street plays, but cinema was unlike anything else she had ever seen or heard. They gave her new songs to sing, new words to utter, and new ways to kill time. She used to come back home and enact scenes from the film out to her friends. Her brothers would play Anji, Surasena, Sajadapa, the king and the queen of Ujjayani – all the secondary characters – but she would play Thota Ramudu, Indumati and Nepala Mantrikudu.

Eleven times. That's how many times she watched *Pathala Bhairavi* in the theatre. And she says that was far fewer than the number of times most other people had watched it. The film was the first of many for her – first film, first story she heard that didn't have a moral, first time she knew how to escape hot afternoons and not stay at home and, most importantly for her and a lot of Telugu people, her first Hero.

The people who love their vowels, accepted a curly haired twenty-seven-year-old Rama Rao as NTR, a star whose acronym has no vowels, as their first Hero.

When Heroes Punch

My grandmother loved this peculiarly Telugu dish called 'Uggani Bajji'. It's a delicious spicy breakfast made with puffed rice and loaded with tomatoes, onions, peanuts, served with chillies fried in batter, akin to fritters. Like a daily soap, the breakfast reduced my grandmother to tears, and yet, she would eat two servings with four bajjis. It's popular in southern Andhra Pradesh, the four districts collectively known as Rayalaseema or Ceded Districts, because they were ceded to the British administrators by the Nizam rulers. Red soil, spicy food, and a violent history that informed the two decades to come after – the region was a favourite setting for Telugu films to create a myth around a Hero.

It is one such tale of a Hero that my grandmother and I went to see in the city of Kurnool. The film was called *Okkadu*. My grandmother was adamant that we watch it in Kurnool, because the film was set there and the experience of watching it in that city would be unparalleled. And because, according to her, the best Uggani Bajji is available in that city. Taking an inter-district bus, after a three-hour journey, we watched *Okkadu,* starring Mahesh Babu. *After* having two servings of Uggani Bajji that reduced us to tears.

The film had already been declared a smash hit, and Mahesh Babu had gone from being the son of a former superstar to himself being a star. He had tried everything before getting there – a grand debut with a star director, a tragic love story, a family film where the threat of him dying at the end seemed real. He had even tried reviving the dead cowboy Western genre. Nothing gave him the stardom he needed. Like my grandmother and I, he had to come to Kurnool – the arid city where the sun's heat is stuffed into its Uggani Bajji.

The single screen theatre was a scary place at first, as it was filled with young, delirious men celebrating the success of the film. Even though it had been nearly three months since its release, the hysteria had not died. As usual, the queue for tickets was shorter for the ladies', so we managed to quickly make our way in and settle into balcony seats. Age had eaten into the sponge of the blue-seat cushions. A family of four, having just escaped the swarm of young men, settled down next to us. They became our allies, and the woman confessed to my grandmother that she was a Mahesh Babu fan, because of his baby-faced looks and fair skin. She looked disappointedly at her husband – a misplaced moustache and a receding hairline that made the man's head resemble the horns of a young bull. But he promised my grandmother that he would get snacks for me – spicy and salted fryums and cola. He must have been a kind man.

The doors were shut, and the lights were turned off. When the titles rolled, the atmosphere became electric. He was not yet Mahesh Babu, just Mahesh. A hundred young men seemed to have been induced into a psychosis at the appearance of his name. The title of the film carved itself on the screen – sheets of light creeping through the blackness on the screen, forming the title in its trademark angular font. The hundred men became at least two hundred, if not more. For those in the balcony seats, mostly families and old people like my grandmother, there were two performances – the film and the celebration of the young men below as they whistled and hooted. When Mahesh Babu finally emerged on-screen, the youth of Kurnool screamed in unison. I barely heard any of the dialogues after that.

Okkadu is a film about Ajay, a young aspiring police officer and Kabaddi player, who goes to Kurnool for a match and crosses path with a local gangster forcing himself on a young girl in the middle of Kurnool. It isn't just *any* place in Kurnool. It's opposite the iconic Konda Reddy Buruju or Konda Reddy Fort. The fort is named after its last ruler, who managed to escape through the secret tunnels known only to him and his family, after the nawabs had imprisoned him. The fort has that kind of legacy. It's part-myth, part-history – melding to become 'folk'. Just like Konda Reddy, another folk legend was being made on the screen.

The villain, played by Prakash Raj, is a tormentor of women and happy families in south India. In Telugu films, villains aren't just bad guys, they are *rakshasa*s. Called Obul Reddy, Prakash Raj's villain in *Okkadu*, was perhaps based on the real-life gangster named Obul Reddy, in the neighbouring district of Anantapur, who was known for his atrocities against women. The people in Kurnool knew the dark context of what was being depicted on-screen.

At one point in the film, Prakash Raj's Obul Reddy is in peak form opposite Konda Reddy Buruju, doing what he does to hapless young women. Ajay walks up to Reddy and punches him, sending him crashing into a transformer. It bursts, and there is a shower of electric sparks that adorn Mahesh Babu's towering frame, as music director Mani Sharma's pulsating background score reverberates across the theatre. A character – a passer-by in the background – on-screen says, 'Someone can hit Obul Reddy in broad daylight on the road, opposite Konda Reddy Buruju! Who the hell is this guy?' Another says, 'He's definitely not from here.' As the audience erupts in the theatre, on-screen, opposite Konda Reddy Buruju in Kurnool, the actor Mahesh emerges as the star Mahesh Babu.

The reason I describe *Okkadu* in so much detail is because the film borrows liberally from *Pathala Bhairavi*. For one, the villain in this film, too, is smitten by the heroine. He seems to genuinely want to impress her and marry her. He calls her *Bangaaru*, the Telugu term of endearment, equating a loved one to gold. In another kind of Telugu film, he would have been the Hero. Off-screen, Prakash Raj was being compared to S.V. Ranga Rao, the man who could play the villain and still come out winning the audience over.

At some point in the second half, much like Nepala Mantrikudu, Prakash Raj kidnaps the Swapna, the heroine played by Bhoomika

Chawla. It feels that the Hero, Mahesh Babu's Ajay, will never find his way back to her. Both Ajay and Swapna are prisoners in their own way – her, dressed up like a bride; him, locked in a prison. And then, straight out of the *Pathala Bhairavi* textbook, Swapna challenges Obul Reddy. 'If you really want me to marry you, fight Ajay like a man and then marry me.'

It is the same attack on masculinity that Indumati inflicted on Nepala Mantrikudu. In retaliation, here, Obul Reddy brings out Ajay to prove himself in front of the heroine. But while taking the Hero back to the marriage hall, Reddy stops at a random spot to kill him. At this point, he is asked the one question that confirms all suspicions about the film's likeness to *Pathala Bhairavi*.

'Have you seen *Pathala Bhairavi*?' Ajay asks Reddy.

'Ten times,' he replies.

Ajay compares himself to Thota Ramudu and warns Reddy that just like in that film, he will kill the Mantrikudu here. Reddy does not like the comparison and orders his men to surround Ajay. Taking a leaf out of Anji from *Pathala Bhairavi*, Ajay's friends surround Obul Reddy and his men.

That is the effect the folklore film has on Telugu cinema grammar even today. Almost all Telugu Heroes are folk heroes, and all villains are folk villains. There are princesses waiting to be rescued. And the Hero's friends are reincarnations of Anjis. The templates, the set-ups and pay-offs that *Pathala Bhairavi* used have crept into the successful and the unsuccessful Telugu films that we see today. Its conversion of folk Heroes and themes into cinematic expressions laid down a formula to be replicated by younger stars, to try and reach new levels of Heroism in pop-imagination.

It's not just the odd film that refers to the text set up by Patala Bhairavi. Telugu cinema's greatest churner of stars and heroes, S.S. Rajamouli, also draws liberally from the tropes set up by the film. It starts with the most basic and mundane things, like the most common name for the female lead in his films being 'Indu', Bhoomika Chawla's character in *Simhadri*, who stabs NTR Jr in the heart-wrenching twist before the intermission; the college student torn between two rivalrous departments, played by Genelia D'Souza, in the rugby-themed action – drama *Sye* (Challenge). In his ambitious reincarnation drama *Magadheera* (Legendary Warrior), Kajal Aggarwal, in her current life, is called Indu. In his most outrageous masala film, *Eega* (Fly), the micro-sculpture artist played by Samantha is called Bindu.

But the more liberal use of *Pathala Bhairavi's* tropes are found in Rajamouli's magnum opus – *Baahubali*. According to Adoor Gopalakrishnan, the National Award-winning Malayalam filmmaker, the *Baahubali* franchise is – for the lack of a better word – a parody of *Pathala Bhairavi*, folk elements being common to both the films. Prabhas' Sivudu has much in common with Thota Ramudu. Both films begin with their respective mothers praying to the gods their sons are named after, to take care of the carefree and troublesome boys. The sequence in *Baahubali* where Sivudu first enters the palace by climbing its walls and roams its grounds by confusing the soldiers is staged like the setup in *Pathala Bhairavi*. While *Baahubali* uses the sequence for dramatic ends, *Pathala Bhairavi* uses it for comical pay-offs between Surasena and Thota Ramudu.

It wouldn't be unreasonable to predict that in Rajamouli's *RRR*, NTR Jr's character will share the wildness and brashness of NTR's Thota Ramudu from *Pathala Bhairavi*.

Pathala Bhairavi, by providing a cinematic medium to folk themes and expressions, created a certain appetite peculiar to the Telugu audience: it took folk stories' penchant for exaggerations and gave them literal forms. This is the reason Telugu cinema Heroes can perform outlandish feats, such as hitting villains and goons to send them flying, punching walls so they crumble to dust, and other such physics-defying sequences that may seem awkward or silly to non-native watchers of Telugu cinema.

How can someone hit like that? That's so unrealistic. To this, the Telugu audience's retort is, *Everyone is aware of that.* The exaggeration is an unspoken contract between the storyteller and audience. Often, when narrating stories from the Mahabharata, a common method used by grandparents to describe Bheema, the second and mightiest Pandava, would be to describe his appetite. The phrase used would be:

Bheemudu bandedu annam thinevaadu
Bheema would eat a cart full of rice.

This is not to say that Bheema could *really* eat that much rice, but the sentence is used to convey how much he could eat, how much he loved rice, how strong he was and so on. The best way to make sense of this tendency for exaggerated images in Telugu cinema is to imagine the director and screenplay writer narrating the story to th audience as if it were a storytelling night at a family gathering or a festival, with nothing but their words to fuel the imagination of listeners. No sound effects, no lights, no actors ... just words.

In this context, *Baahubali* is a great example. The film spends the first half hour trying to establish Sivudu's ambition of climbing a seemingly insurmountable waterfall, which seems to stretch into the heavens. The storyteller wants to tell us two things: one, that beyond the waterfall lies adventure which Sivudu seeks; and two, that Sivudu, the son of Baahubali, has mighty powerful arms. He has tried a thousand times since he was a child to climb the waterfall but with minimal success. As he grows older, he manages to climb a little higher than before, but no amount of dedication, will and strength seems enough to surmount this waterfall ... until a wooden mask of a young woman makes its way down the waterfall and lands in the hands of Sivudu. At this point, one can imagine a storyteller narrating it thus:

Sivudu now wanted to climb the waterfall more than ever. He made up his mind, his will was stronger than the strongest rock in all the land where the sun could reach. He wanted to meet the woman behind this mask. Even if she was in the land above the waterfall. Even if, like his mother told him, there were ghosts and demons on the other side. Sivudu made up his mind to climb the waterfall. At first, he slipped. Even the water seemed to fall harder that day than any other day. He climbed rock by rock. He could only think of her. Who is she? His arms ached, but he pushed himself onwards with all his might; he would even push the mountain down if he had to. He would reach her. When he was tired, he would often see her apparition – like a ghost. Maybe his mother was right. At one point, he reached a dead end – even his sinewy arms couldn't handle this. It was a distance that stretched from that house over there to at least ten houses away from it. Nobody could jump that far, not even Sivudu. The water had more force than a thousand elephants running. He had never seen anything like it.

'How did he jump that far then?' someone from the crowd would ask.

'If it was you or me, we would have died of fear. Or come back home. But not Sivudu. He tore a small branch out of a tree. Collecting old twigs that were washing down. He made a small bow for himself. He then took a small sharp rock, sharper than a needle, and tied it to a stick to make an arrow.'

'Why a bow and arrow?' another would ask.

'Far away, there was one tree. If he jumped, and released the bow at the right time, the arrow would get stuck and he would hang to the tree. And then he could climb up.'

'What if he doesn't hit the tree?'

'Death. He would fall off like dust through the roof. So Sivudu took the bow and arrow. He knew what he had to do. He had to look at nothing but the tree. His brain told him about the girl. He pushed the thought away.'

Someone would interject again. 'What about his mother?'

'If he thought about her, he would fail. He pushed that thought away like it was a fly in the summer. He took one step back and jumped off the rock he was standing on, and mid-air, he released the arrow. And like a fast tiger, the arrow pounced on to the tree and locked itself. Sivudu was safe. And with the last burst of energy in him, he finally climbed the waterfall – his childhood dream. His arms had carried him so far. But it was his love for the woman behind the mask that would take him further into this land. Are there ghosts? Are there princesses? Are there horses? Sivudu crossed the river to find out.

The storyteller would then proceed to tell the rest of the story with similarly exaggerated metaphors and similes. It is not to infantilize the Telugu audience that filmmakers resort to these techniques. There is an implicit understanding that these are exaggerated metaphors, similes and personifications that find an audio-visual form. This isn't applicable only to mythological or fantasy films.

Even a rightly criticized film such as *Arjun Reddy*, for all its misogynistic undertones, devotes a good proportion of its time to creating a myth around the protagonist's anger. 'Arjun's temper, like a volcano, could make him talk back to the dean of his college. Arjun was starved for sex.' 'How starved?' you ask. 'Enough to shove ice cubes into his pants in the middle of the road. In full public view.'

This way of using images subverts the idea that art should imitate life. These techniques focus on the idea that art *exaggerates* life, and the audience is sensible enough to know that. *Pathala Bhairavi* didn't just give the Telugu audience its first folk Hero, it gave rise to the idea that all heroes are essentially folk heroes. It throws a challenge at the actors succeeding NTR: *The audiences already know life, but can you take them beyond it?*

The quest to answer this question has since shaped the way stardom is chased and understood by Telugu actors – whether Prabhas, with his mountain-like frame, or a fair-skinned Mahesh Babu, with a baby face that impressed the married woman who sat next to me in Kurnool.

Who Does a Hero Fantasize About?

Once upon a time, before there were Starbucks, democracies and planes, there lived a young man called Manisiddhudu who wanted to visit Kashi. As a conservative Hindu man, visiting Kashi was an important task in his bucket list. Given that this journey of nearly 1,300 kilometres across mountains, rivers, forests and strange lands would be a scary prospect, he wanted company. He asked everyone he knew, and none said yes. 'Dacoits, ghosts, scary monsters await,' they argued. 'It is a mad endeavour,' they said. 'If you want to see your God, wait for old age.' But Manisiddhudu was hell-bent on going on this journey. And finally, after weeding through hundreds, he found one young man who was willing to come, but on one condition: whatever happens, he must be entertained along the journey; else, he would return home. With no other option, Manisiddhudu concocts stories about moral conduct, values, valour and bravery, friendship, princes and princesses, kings and kingdoms, good and evil, all the way until they reach Kashi.

This is the premise of *Kaasi Majili Kathalu* (Stories told en-route to Kashi), a collection of folk stories, codified later by Madhira Subbanna Deekshithulu. One of the stories from within *Kaasi Majili Kathalu* gave birth to *Pathala Bhairavi*. The setup of *Kaasi Majili Kathalu* is similar to that of *1001 Arabian Nights*, in which a queen sentenced to death tells 1001 stories to the king to postpone her eventual death. A larger framework is set up to tell multiple short stories with endearing characters. While *Arabian Nights* features Aladdin, Sindbad and Alibaba, in the stories of *Kaasi Majili Kathalu*, Thota Ramudu appears. A similar set up is used in Geoffrey Chaucer's *Canterbury Tales*, in which pilgrims travelling from London to Canterbury compete to tell the best story to win a free meal at an inn, and in the Italian film *The Decameron*, stories are told by young men and women trapped in a villa outside Florence to escape the Black Death.

Pathala Bhairavi isn't the only film to come out of *Kaasi Majili Kathalu*. NTR's other folklore fantasy *Gulebakavali Katha* (The Story of the Gulebakavali Flower) was extracted from it as well, as was *Keelu gurram* (The Magical Horse) and *Sahasra Sricheda Apoorva Chintamani* (The Extraordinary Chintamani Who Took a Thousand

Lives). All these are swashbuckler films, involving rightful heirs to thrones sword-fighting their way to the top, damsels in distress and demons. The lead of *Sahasra Sricheda Apoorva Chintamani*, Kantha Rao, came to be known as Kattula Kanta Rao (sword-wielding Kanta Rao) because of this film and many other similar films he acted in.

But it isn't just early cinema that borrowed from Telugu folk culture. Folk tales have given rise to genres within Telugu cinema that are not found elsewhere. One such is the *attha–alludu*. To those who are not from the Telugu-speaking regions, it will perhaps sound strange. *Attha* and *alludu* translate to mother-in-law and son-in-law, respectively. It borrows elements from the culture where the mother-in-law and the son-in-law share a faux-flirtatious relationship, while using the trope of taming the shrew. The genre stems from folk songs that deviate from the sanitized understanding of sacred relationships within a family setting. Some examples of these relationships are between brothers-in-law and sisters-in-law, modelled after Lakshaman-Sita relationship in the Ramayana; or between the daughters-in-law and the parents-in-law, modelled after Sita and Draupadi, in the Ramayana and Mahabharata, respectively, where obedience is expected from the wife.

An example of this flirtatious relationship between the mother-in-law and the son-in-law can be found in the Telangana folk song 'Ennadu Raani Alludoche' (The Son-in-Law Who Barely Visits Has Finally Come Home). The song is a duet and a dialogue between the mother-in-law and the son-in-law, who is missing his wife because she has returned to her parents' house having fallen ill.

The husband tries to plead with his mother-in-law to let his wife come back, and the mother-in-law placates the antsy husband. He is even suffering from a terrible cold and fever, he tells her. She first asks if he wants to eat fancy white rice or the locally available millet. The demanding son-in-law chooses the fancy white rice, because he is feeling sick and needs some food that will rejuvenate him. Then she asks him if he wants chicken or mutton, and not one to shy away from demanding the best for himself, the young man asks for mutton. Now the two of them have become comfortable, and the man seems to have forgotten the original purpose of his visit. He asks her for something to drink. She coyly asks if he prefers lime soda or a cola, and he says he prefers alcohol. She then gives him a choice: beer or brandy? He obviously prefers brandy. For his fever, of course.

Then she asks if he wants a bed or a mat to sleep on. He says he'll be uncomfortable on a mat, so he prefers a nice comfortable bed. Then the man awkwardly approaches his mother-in-law and once again asks her to send her daughter back so she can take care of him. The mother-in-law replies that she can't send her daughter because she is worried that he will spread the illness to her. The man asks if there is any way out, and the mother-in-law comes up with a solution. It might be tricky, she warns him. She asks if he's the kind of man to feel shy, to which he confidently replies that he's not.

Finally, she drops the bomb. The only solution is if she goes home with her son-in-law. Without missing a beat, the young man happily agrees. He says the daughter might be inexperienced and will scream, so he'd much rather have his mother-in-law. And voila, his fever has disappeared at the prospect of his mother-in-law coming home. He poses one final question to the listeners, asking if any young man will ever fall sick if such a mother-in-law exists in their lives.

While traditional understanding dictates that these relationships toe rigid lines, their porous nature seeps through in folk songs like these. In social practice, daughters do marry their young uncles (typically mother's youngest brother) and brothers marry the widow of their deceased brothers – but these barely ever make it to mainstream stories. The reasons for these practices range from natural attraction between consenting adults to caste-based rigid practices to securing property within households by negating the consent of the women.

The *attha–alludu* genre of films borrows the liberal bent from these songs but uses it as a weapon for the hero against his in-laws.

Films in this genre were particularly popular late '80s and early '90s. Like the men these films depicted, the film industry had reached a middle age by then, set in its ways, and the first generation of star children had begun to make their mark. The industry had moved away from the hands of producers to the demands of stars. The first Hero, NTR, had gone on to become the chief minister, and a new Hero, Chiranjeevi, had taken his place as the emperor of Telugu cinema.

Villains, too, were getting boring. NTR had defeated all the mythological villains; Krishna – Mahesh Babu's father, popularly known as Superstar Krishna – had taken on the system as an angry young man; Shobhan Babu, another star who was popular among ladies, had defeated all the villains at the village level; while Chiranjeevi and the other younger heroes had defeated urban villains like mafia dons, industrialists and politicians. The wicked were being destroyed, and the only novel way to deal with villains now was to show evil being transformed. But that would frustrate the audience and not allow for the necessary catharsis.

And so, the film industry turned to the feisty mother-in-law.

The 'feisty' mother-in-law trope was not new. Yesteryear actress Suryakantham was popular for taking on several such roles. She terrorized the women in the audience, making them pray that they never get a mother-in-law like that. Sons wouldn't want a dominating mother like that either. Husbands would pray to all the gods that they wouldn't get such wives, or their daughter such in-laws. Every husband who was cast opposite her was henpecked. My mother used to call my grandmother Suryakantham, that's how legendary she was. In Suryakantham's most memorable role, Gundamma in *Gundamma Katha* (*Gundamma's Story*), her sons-in-law were NTR and ANR – the two biggest stars at that point of time. And their father? S.V. Ranga Rao. It took Telugu cinema's biggest heroes to tame the 'shrew' that was Suryakantham. That's how much she popularized the role of the feisty mother-in-law – one that was evil but could eventually be tamed.

What changed in the late '80s and '90s? Of course, there was generally a dearth of potential villains to pit against Heroes. Then, the first generation of female actors who had acted opposite NTR and ANR had aged, but were still eager for roles. Once considered sex symbols, they were too old to play sisters and sisters-in-law. They could be cast as the villainous mother-in-law pitted against new heroes, while still being sexualized on-screen, unlike Suryakantham, who was born on cinema as the mother-in-law and whose popularity only began in her later years.

The creation of this genre also attracted an older generation of film watchers, who had stopped going to the theatres after the '70s, when 'their' Heroes had started looking aged and awkward in front of the younger crop. The older heroines in this new genre would bring more than sexuality; they would represent the aspirations of a bygone generation. For the older generation, it was a victory of sorts: *The youth might be ruling the roost, but they would have to put up a fight, and we will dance and sing with them while we go down.* The most popular actor to play 'attha' was actress Vanisri, who had perfected the role of the arrogant young woman opposite NTR and ANR, and was now ready to battle the younger crop of Heroes. Same arrogance, different roles.

The attha–alludu genre of films had a set template and its core structure was simple. A rich woman with a henpecked husband raises wayward daughters – mostly two, sometimes one – who are arrogant, brash, modern, and miniature versions of herself. To defeat the lower-class Hero, who is uncouth, sexist and conservative in his outlook, the *attha* joins hands with the wrong kind of men, who are also uncouth and sexist, but belong to an upper class and caste. Through trick, song, and fight, the Hero defeats the people who led his mother-in-law and her daughters down a wayward path, setting his mother-in-law straight. A changed person, the *attha* now promises to be a 'good' submissive wife. Before the Hero can decide which of the daughters he's in love with, if not both, the film ends.

This is the broad plot that most films in the genre followed. Crammed into the film was almost always a song where the Hero dances not only with the lead actresses, but also with his mother-in-law – gyrating, slapping her posterior, lip-syncing to double meaning lyrics.

The peak of this genre was the 1995 film *Alluda Majaka* (No one Entertains like the Son-in-Law), a film starring Chiranjeevi, Rambha and Ramya Krishnan. Lakshmi played the mother-in-law. The film is a sleaze-fest and probably the sleaziest of all of Chiranjeevi's works. There are films that age badly, and there are those that are terrible even at the time they are released. This was one of them. A chunk of the second half of the film's plot revolves around the villain 'raping' a woman – except the woman falsely accusing the villain is a comedy actor in drag. This isn't far from being the cringiest scene in the film. In another scene, Chiranjeevi's character, Sitaramudu, is locked in a room with the two lead heroines and the mother-in-law, and then the lights go out. The women scream, and when the lights come back on, all their blouses are torn. Sitaramudu is seen relishing what he's done. The film thinks it's being cheeky and later tries to argue that the Hero actually did not do anything, but by then it's too late. Then there is a dream sequence in which Chiranjeevi dances with his wife, sister-in-law and mother-in-law. All of them are dressed in equally skimpy clothes. The stanza dedicated to the mother-in-law talks about him pinching, scratching and tickling her. The sequence accurately captures the level of sleaze in the film.

Alluda Majaka caused such controversy that for the first time people protested against Chiranjeevi. Women's groups complained to the Central Board of Film Certification (CBFC) to have the film removed from theatres because of how obscene it was. This film caused the right wing to join the cause of the left wing in the demand for its ban. The Bharatiya Mahila Morcha ensured the issue was raised in the Legislative Assembly. Coming to Chiranjeevi's rescue were his fans who threatened to commit suicide if the film was

revoked or stopped from being released in theatres. All of this was
compounded by the fact that this was Chiranjeevi, the first family-
friendly Hero. While NTR was a favourite among young men and
ANR was a favourite among the ladies, Chiranjeevi was loved by
families. Children, mothers, fathers, grandparents ... everyone loved
him.

None of the themes in this film were new, going by Chiranjeevi's
filmography. He had tormented a mother-in-law before in *Attaku
Yamudu Ammayiki Mogudu* (God of Death to the Mother-in-law but
Husband to the Girl); he had escaped a prison like he does in the early
parts of *Alluda Majaka* in *Khaidi* (Prisoner); and he had even played
the young man who represents the interests of the downtrodden in
the biggest hit of his career, *Gharana Mogudu* (Rogue Husband).
Yet, *Alluda Majaka* was seen as a betrayal, because nobody expected
this level of explicit immorality from Chiranjeevi. The director of the
film, E.V.V. Satyanarayana, had experimented in this genre before, in
a film titled *Allari Alludu* (The Naughty Son-in-Law), and it had not
received this sort of flak.

Around this time, Chiranjeevi was coming off a couple of flops
after hitting the highest point of stardom in his career. Until that
point, his stardom had been so legendary that not only was he the
first one to charge ₹1 crore per film in the entire country, but he was
also on the cover of *The Week* with a headline that blared 'BIGGER
THAN BACHCHAN' – *the* Amitabh Bachchan. And Chiranjeevi
had achieved all this in a state cocooned away in South India. A
popular anecdote about the height of his stardom was that he once
visited three different cities across Andhra Pradesh on the same day
in a helicopter to celebrate the success of *Gharana Mogudu*.

After hitting this level of success, he didn't have a hit for two years
must have shaken the man. It doesn't justify *Alluda Majaka*, but it
explains what made Chiranjeevi take up a genre that emerged from
folk roots – something that had given him success before. Despite
all the controversy surrounding it, the film became a massive hit.

Although the *attha–alludu* genre took a beating with its release, it continues to be a tried and tested genre for young actors, even today. NTR Jr, the grandson of NTR, tried it twice in films titled *Allari Ramudu* (Naughty Ramudu) and *Naa Alludu* (My Son-in-Law). The films had Nagma and Ramya Krishnan playing mothers-in-law. Having played the daughters-in-law in such films in the '90s, they had been 'promoted' and now got to dance in a duet with the next generation of Heroes. Even Pawan Kalyan, currently a politician who has apparently bid goodbye to films, resorted to this genre for the biggest hit of his career, in *Attharintiki Daredi* (How do I Get to My Mother-in-Law's House?). Although the film was devoid of any sexual connotations, it retained the 'taming of the shrew' theme of the genre. As recently as 2018, actor Naga Chaitanya unsuccessfully tried his luck with the genre with *Shailaja Reddy Alludu* (Shailaja Reddy's Son-in-Law), hoping for a mass hit. Here, too, Ramya Krishna helped boost the career of a young actor while playing the mother-in-law.

Having criticized *Alluda Majaka*, I must make a confession. This was the first ever film I saw in a theatre. On a scorching and dusty afternoon, my parents had taken me along with my entire family to a small screen in the town of Anantapur. Even my grandmother had come with us. We were still a family of four; my sister hadn't been born yet. We went to the theatre because my mother loved Chiranjeevi, as did my father. My grandmother figured she had found a replacement for NTR. The controversy surrounding the film did not deter them. Indeed, my family wanted to watch the film with a vengeance. They felt that the protests were driven by jealous folks, with the system uniting against a successful and talented actor.

After my father fought away rabid Chiranjeevi fans to obtain tickets, we entered the dingy hall. We didn't get tickets for the seats in the balcony, so we settled for the seats amidst the manic fans, mostly comprising young men. I was all but two years old and had just learnt to walk. I didn't even need a ticket for my first-ever film. Apparently, I wasn't crying despite the clamour around me. My mother, too, was waiting to be taken into another world for three hours before her duties as mother and daughter-in-law resumed.

And then, the film began.

Horrified and disgusted, my parents and grandmother wanted to leave as soon as they understood where the story was headed. There were early warning signs – a scene that shows the heroines bathing in a stream, as the water level recedes around them, while all the men of the village led by Chiranjeevi watch on; jokes about prostitution; a pregnancy that pops out of nowhere and is an excuse to use the vilest insults. Through all this, my parents persisted. Finally, when the scene with the light going off hit the screen, my parents and grandmother were determined to exit the hall.

There was a small problem, though. I had wandered away and was nowhere to be found. My mother started to panic as my dad looked for me. My grandmother was simply livid. Chiranjeevi was cracking misogynistic jokes on-screen, while young men hooted and clapped. My parents continued looking for me, and a small search party banded together –concerned audience members who had been seated around us. Half an hour later, they spotted me wandering next to the screen, surrounded by the same young men they were afraid of. My father walked towards them to rescue me.

And then the song began – the one where Chiranjeevi does things he's not supposed to do to his mother-in-law. When the chorus of the song hit, to the horror of my parents and grandmother, I was gyrating and doing pelvic thrusts at the screen as the amused young men cheered me on. They saw in me the youngest Chiranjeevi fan. One of them apparently put me on his shoulders and the whole theatre erupted to my dancing. Once the song was over, my dad snatched me away from the young man and walked briskly towards the exit, scolding me. My nascent friendship with the stranger was cut short, and my grandmother and mother had a new issue to quarrel over for the next decade or so.

Many dramatic changes happened after *Alluda Majaka*. Chiranjeevi's image took a beating for the first time, postponing his political entry. He was no more the on-screen god he used to be. Nine months later, my sister was born. While until that day, I used to sleep with my parents; after that, my grandmother ensured I slept next to her every day.

I heard the story about the burning bus for the first time that night.

If Heroes Said Thank You

Fairly or unfairly, the benefits of folk tales and culture have accrued to Telugu Heroes. They have garnered applause; they have launched their sons, grandsons, their political careers. Two of the biggest Heroes Telugu cinema has produced needed folk stories and folk subcultures to either establish or save their Herodom. NTR needed the magic of *Pathala Bhairavi*, and Chiranjeevi needed a sultry mother-in-law. This wasn't the last time they'd use these folk stories. NTR, a year before launching his party, would use the part-history and part-folk mythos around the region of Bobbili. This region is touted to have produced fierce warriors who fought against colonial forces. Tales of the historic battle over the Bobbili Fort and the royal families of the region are retold much like the Rajputs and Maratha retelling their tales of war and glory. While there are historical precedents for these events, the stories are told and the heroes valorized through folk mechanisms. NTR created the 'Bobbili' sub-genre, while acting in films like *Bobbili Puli* (The Tiger of Bobbili) and *Bobbili Yuddham* (The War for Bobbili). Other actors, too, became part of this category of films – Krishnam Raju, another Telugu Hero who capitalized on his career in cinema to enter politics, acted in *Bobbili Brahmanna* (Brahmanna of Bobbili); actor Venkatesh had his own version of *Gods Must Be Crazy* in *The Bobbili Raja*.

Recognizing the impact of folk heroes and their importance to Telugu cinema rids it of one important myth – that all mainstream cinema is essentially a retelling of the epics. All good male lead actors are modelled around Ram. All evil villains get a Ravana treatment. And all heroines are reduced to Sita. Telugu cinema's dependence on folk sensibilities resist against such blanket arguments. The epics are great stories in and of themselves, but there are other stories too. This infusion into Telugu cinema is a way of folklore to demarcate space. A Ramudu challenges our understanding of foreigners. *Attha-alludu* tell us the porous nature of supposedly rigid relationships. The markers of differentiation are not limited to cinema and extend to the way the culture of cinema is enjoyed. Films such as *Baahubali* have taken Telugu cinema to an international audience. Matt Groening, the creator of *The Simpsons*, accepts that Rajamouli's *Magadheera* was his inspiration for his new animated show *Disenchantment*. But it's in the small lanes of Guntur on hot afternoons, in crying after eating Uggani Bajji in Kurnool, in singing songs during festivals in Telangana that Telugu cinema finds the stories truly worth telling.

Folk stories are also where Telugu cinema draws its method of exaggerated emotions from. The images on-screen are metaphors and similes used by folk storytellers. There is some irony in the fact that while the culture of folk storytellers arriving in small towns during festivals is quickly disappearing, Telugu stars (who play folk Heroes) and Telugu directors (new substitutes for folk storytellers), compete to release their films around Ugadi and Sankranti, when films get large returns owing to the number of holidays issued by the government.

In the process of trying to chart the graph of these storytellers, I may have done one storyteller gross disservice. My grandmother. *All* her stories weren't bad – because her best one was her last.

I had always wondered what made me my grandmother's favourite grandchild. I wasn't particularly well-behaved, I wasn't academically bright or promising, I wasn't even gifted with cuteness that other children seem to have. What was it that made me – the recipient of her stories and experiences – special?

I eventually did ask her one day. I was hoping that she would negate my insecurities regarding my behaviour, intelligence or looks. Grandmothers tend to be the last resort when one requires compliments. But my grandmother told me a different story. During her youth, all she wanted was someone like NTR in her life. He was the actor she loved more than anybody else. That was the first time she even knew she could fantasize about another man. The man who gave her a reason to escape the clutches of her parents. The man who sang songs under the moonlight. The commoner who would build a palace for the woman he loves.

But she never got to meet the actor her whole life – not even a glimpse. That was her one big regret. She prayed to all the gods she knew, but none conjured up that serendipitous encounter between NTR and his most loyal fan who grew up in Guntur.

I told her how horrible that was and how horrible all the gods are for not listening to her prayers. She concurred.

'But what does that have to with me?'

She replied that after giving up hope, just as a joke, she prayed to another goddess, to see if anything can happen. And the Goddess answered. It wasn't the real deal, but it's the closest any divine entity had ever gotten her to NTR.

In 1993, on 28 May – the very same date on which NTR celebrates his birthday – I was born. In a life where that quest to meet NTR seemed impossible, and futile, this gift was the answer to my grandmother's prayers.

Fictional goddesses can only do so much.

Jai Pathala Bhairavi.

3

Readers Versus Audience: The Great Journey to a New World

I too gave myself as fuel to the world's fire!
I too shed a teardrop for the stream of the world!
I too lent my crazy yells to the noise in the world!
      – *Jayabheri* (Sounds of the Drums of Victory)

Soil and Wounds

When I was leaving home for Mumbai to start life as an aspiring writer, my father gifted me *Mahaprasthanam* (The Great Journey to a New World), a collection of poems by the poet Sri Sri. It was a symbolic gift, meant to ensure that I didn't forget my roots in the pursuit of my dreams. The loaded gesture would have been poignant, had my Telugu vocabulary not been so abysmal. Almost all the poems flew over my head or were lost in translation as I googled word after word. I struggled to make sense of the words, let alone grasp the romantic revolutionary metaphors.

Yet, it was only *partially* my fault that I could not comprehend the layers within the Telugu language. In school, until I was ten years old, I avoided Telugu as much as possible. It wasn't just that I forced myself to think and speak in English, like storing plum jam in a jar meant for mango pickles. Encouraged by my parents, I took Hindi as my second language subject – their logic being that since Telugu was spoken at home, thus guaranteeing fluency, for the price of one year's school fee, I could learn another language. My parents weren't unique in this view, which led to many Telugu-speaking students choosing Hindi as their second language over Telugu.

This ingenious cost-saving tactic led to a love–hate affair with Hindi. The language was particularly elusive because of how deceptively similar it seemed to Telugu, since both borrowed from Sanskrit. But just when I seemed to have grasped the language between my fingers, the gendered nature of Hindi words struck a blow at my confidence. Strilling and purling – so easy and organic for native Hindi speakers – felt devoid of logic coming on the back of a language like Telugu with no such pretensions. How could words even have a gender?

But I persisted.

I even took part in a stage adaptation of the play *Jamun Ka Ped* (Jamun Tree). A satire on the Indian bureaucracy, the story is about a poet trapped underneath a jamun tree, unable to get help because of the bureaucracy involved in getting the tree removed. Each wing of the government finds itself asking a layer above it for more permissions, while finding new obstacles and reasons to not move the tree off the poet's back. Eventually, the poet dies, not under the weight of the tree but under that of the Indian bureaucracy. All the king's horses and all the Indian government's paperwork couldn't lift a tree to save a dying man. A wonderful play that got an equally wonderful applause from the school management and other students. I did audition for a bigger part, but I didn't get a speaking role because like a foot on a lotus leaf, my mouth could not stand confidently on the Hindi words.

The teacher laughed at my Hindi and felt best to give me the task of carrying the tree and placing it on the stage before the play began. In the next few years, more such humiliations accrued.

I persisted still.

Then I got my marks. First, seven out of twenty-five. Then seven out of fifty. Then six out of twenty-five. And then in 2003, I saw the Telugu film *Simhadri* starring NTR Jr in one of the first multiplex-like theatres in Anantapur, where tickets were more expensive, and they sold popcorn in plastic containers instead of fryums and onion samosas wrapped in paper. It's a film by S.S. Rajamouli, the director of the *Baahubali* franchise. He was a younger director then, which meant his technical abilities were raw and many of his scenes were 'ideas'. One knew what he was trying to say even if they didn't translate fully. And not having the attention of national or international media to rein him in meant he was unhinged in some portions of the film.

NTR Jr had seen a tremendous rise in his stardom. He had started acting as a lead in films when he was seventeen and had two blockbusters, *Student No. 1* and *Aadi*. But *Simhadri* wasn't just any hit film; it was such a big hit that there was even talk of him entering politics and campaigning for the political party started by his grandfather – the Telugu Desam Party. There was a glimpse of what his grandfather, NTR, did to inspire Telugu pride. He was nineteen at the time. The subtext could have been a film by itself.

There's a scene in the film that has no business inspiring the mind of a ten-year-old boy struggling with Hindi and avoiding Telugu. But it did that to me anyway.

Simhadri, who has led a secret life as a vigilante-gangster called Singamalai in Kerala, has destroyed the tyrannical criminal empire of Bhaisaab, the primary antagonist. He's even killed Bhaisaab's brother and sent Bhaisaab to jail. The actor playing the villain is an 'outsider'. It's Mukesh Rishi in a cheap wig that looks more like tentacles sprouting of his scalp. It was the beginning of a new phase of villains in Telugu cinema; the south Indian varieties having been exhausted, villains were being imported from other states. Homegrown 'villains', such as Kota Srinivasa Rao, or other south Indian variants such as Prakash Raj, did the odd film where they played a troubled father, a supportive husband, or a funny brother; it was tough to believe that he could be purely evil. Mukesh Rishi had no such baggage; slap on a moustache and make him glare with his big expressive eyes, and every audience member wanted him dead, vanquished.

The scene of interest is the climactic battle between the hero and the villain, which takes place outside a hospital. I use the word 'battle' deliberately over the word 'fight'. It's not two men fighting over women, land or, even, egos. There are hordes of men wielding sickles and axes. There are bombs being hurled. Simhadri has been hospitalized, Bhaisaab has been released from jail and he wants revenge. He is ready to kill the man. Simhadri, despite having bandages around his chest, and Bhaisaab meet on the battlefield. They kick, punch, kill those in their way as if they were mosquitoes on a cold winter day. Blood is spilling around them, making the red soil even redder. The background music amplifies Simhadri's anger, but also punctuates every punch from the hero. The fight between Mukesh Rishi and NTR Jr reminds one of a fight between lions on the Discovery channel.

When it seems like it's a clash between equals, Bhaisaab punches Simhadri in the chest, causing him to bleed and fall to the ground. The villain has the upper hand. It's a scene that's been played out countless times before. Everyone knows the hero will eventually fight back and win. But what prompts Simhadri to fight through his bleeding wound? What makes the hero, who has been temporarily knocked unconscious, *conscious*?

Bhaisaab says the unthinkable as he begins to kick and punch Simhadri, who is out of both breath and the will to live. 'Show me your Telugu pride.' A punch to the face. 'Where is the Andhra masculinity you bragged about?' Another punch, and Simhadri spits blood out of his mouth. A few more punches and kicks later, Bhaisaab says the worst thing that could have been uttered to a Telugu Hero: '*Is this all the power there is in your Telugu soil?*' Bhaisaab then spits on the soil, while a son of the soil lies on the ground, bleeding to death.

If Mukesh Rishi had walked into the theatre that day, people might have forgotten he was just an actor.

From the red dust around him, Simhadri rises. The background music consisting of violins and synthesizers and drums plays like a soft tremor on water, sending ripples of power across the auditorium. Bhaisaab is taken aback. He thought Simhadri was done. Maybe he was, but the last insult to the Telugu pride did something to Simhadri. As a ten-year-old, I was simmering with anger, too. Simhadri picks up a fistful of red soil. The background music explodes like a fountain. He takes the soil and rubs his wound with it. On his chest. A bomb explodes in background causing a tornado of dancing red soil. The background music competes with it. The theatre goes bonkers. Drums and synthesizers compete with the violence on-screen. Simhadri stands and bears a few more punches. But this time, he's unfazed. The wound and the soil seem to be doing their thing. And now, it's Simhadri's turn. He doesn't just punch Bhaisaab back. There is a punchline waiting.

'*Do you really want to see the power in Andhra's soil?*'

When NTR Jr says this in his gravelly voice, it is menacing. It causes the young men in the theatres to tear their shirts and toss them up in the air like it was a graduating ceremony. It was – not theirs , but NTR Jr's. He's laid the foundation for his claim to be a Hero. He's not just a star anymore. He is a Hero, at the age of nineteen, defending Telugu pride, like his grandfather once did. There is a subtext to the punch and the punchlines. This unlikely scene inspired Telugu pride in the ten-year-old me, and I decided to quit Hindi as a second language and pursue Telugu instead. My marks in Hindi made an easy case to convince my parents, but it took a villain from Kerala to stab NTR Jr for me to learn Telugu and understand it. But I was the only one. Other Telugu-speaking students who took Hindi persisted.

They didn't see what the Andhra soil could do to wounded egos and chests. They weren't in Anantapur watching *Simhadri*.

Is ours a life worth living?
Like dogs, like foxes!
Is ours a life worth living?
Like pigs on the streets
It's true, it's true,
What you said is true!
Life is a shadow, education is a shadow,
Poems are a bitter fruit!

— *Chedu Paata* (The Bitter Song)

God Must Be a Hero

As a language, Telugu is younger than Tamil and Sanskrit, creating a unique set of problems for its writers. The Telugu-speaking regions have existed as a bridge between the Dravidian forces to their south, while being open to the winds from the north — giving the language a distinct flavour that has added to its lexicon, words and works from both regions. This is also reflected in the number of religions that have occupied central space in the region. Buddhism and Jainism dominated the region comprising the Telugu states before the first-known concrete works of the Telugu literature were produced. The almost-capital Amaravati and several Buddhist stupas in the north-east districts of Srikakulam are testimony to their influence. Later, different sects of Hinduism, such as Shaivism, Vaishnavism, Madhavism and Advaitism, dictated popular belief. With the fall of the Vijayanagara dynasty and the arrival of the Nizams, Islam spread across the region, while the British Empire left an imprint of Christianity in the state. The practitioners of the Telugu language have been influenced across these different, larger forces of history. While historians have not found any codified form of the language from the days when Jainism and Buddhism held the popular imagination, they have been able to trace it from the point in history when more recognizably Hindu gods started to command the belief of the people.

It is in this context that, starting around 1100 AD, writers and poets emerged. They have been historically split for three broad purposes. First, as writers and storytellers who could write the seminal religious texts of the time that preserve gods and perpetuate myths. These writers would lead lives of asceticism and saintliness, devoted and dedicated to one god. Second, writers who lived under the patronage of a king and contributed in creating hagiographies for the king. If a writer dedicated a work to a king, it meant the king was immortalized for posterity. Unlike the modern connotation of the word 'dedication', which would be in the early pages of a book as an indulgence for the writer, ancient dedications were for the king to whom the book and the verses were addressed. Srinatha, the royal Telugu poet, was 'given a bath in gold' by having gold coins poured over him as a reward for dedicating his book to a king. Kings survived through the stories that were constructed about them. It is no coincidence that Krishna Deva Raya, the writer-poet, is also the region's most remembered king. Later, a third species emerged, who were the progressive writers that pushed the boundaries of society towards to a liberal future. These writers became more prominent in the nineteenth century.

And in the last fifty years, another new breed of writers has emerged – *the Telugu film writers*. Writers of Telugu films are useful creatures. They can take an ordinary man who looks like he could be anybody on the street – average height, average build – and make them seem god-like. Take someone like Chiranjeevi, who has prided himself in being the son of a police constable who's risen to the top of the cinema food chain. Telugu people believe that he is the undisputed 'king' of the box office. They even use the word *simhasanam* (throne) when speaking of his power over the box-office. If we remove the stardom and the baggage, Chiranjeevi could be the guy behind a counter in the bank. The person busily buying eggs, while he rushes back to his awkwardly parked car. But once he gives life to the screenplays of Paruchuri Brothers, the duo who set the template for Hero films for decades, Chiranjeevi is almost a God. In his 2002 film *Indra*, donning an easily identifiable wig and cheap lipstick, he warns the villain – it's Mukesh Rishi again. It's a familiar sequence of good vs evil. God vs demon. A man who is worshipped by his people going against the embodiment of an evil vulture. This good man who mostly looks like you and me, through one dialogue is transformed into a god: *Simhasanam meedha koorchune arhate akkada aa Indrudidhi. Ikkada ee Indra Senudidhi.* (The throne in heaven is for the king of gods, Indra. And this throne is for the man standing in front of you.) Suddenly, you believe him. It's a terrific performance. The background score feels like it dropped from the heavens too. But there's magic in the dialogue, in the set up. The situation that has been concocted makes the cheesy line feel apt to the audience of Telugu cinema. It's all in the writing; it makes Chiranjeevi the king of the gods for a few seconds. *That's a few seconds more than most people.*

This breed of writers, the film writers, has managed to put at serious risk any other form of writing. Why read when you can indulge in watching something deliciously spicy? Why go for the subtle when instant gratification is so easily available? Why waste hours reading a book when you can get emotionally burnt out through a two-and-a-half-hour film?

According to the All India Survey on Higher Education, a 2015–16 report published by the Department of Higher Education of the Ministry of Human Resource Development, the total number of enrolments at the PhD level in the discipline of Telugu language and literature is 167 out of the nearly 7,000 enrolments in all the Indian languages (a mere 2 per cent). Tamil had 236 enrolments and Urdu and Sanskrit had 425 and 571, respectively. This, coupled with the fact that the total number of PhDs awarded that year in the discipline of Telugu language and literature stood at a total of only 27 students, gives an insight into the status of engagement with the language.

While the number of PhDs may not accurately reflect the readership, it is indicative of the level of engagement.

Telugu is neither a nascent language trying to find its feet nor spoken by a fast-disappearing minority. A significant number of the songs of the Carnatic music tradition are composed in Telugu, perhaps because the ease with which syllables can roll off the tongue give it an innate musicality. There are two famous quotes about the Telugu language. One from Krishna Deva Raya, who remarked (in Telugu), '*Deshabhashalandu Telugu lessa*', which roughly translates to 'Of all the languages in the nation, Telugu is the best.' The emperor himself contributed to the language through his epic poem, *Amuktamalyada*. Telugu was the language of the court for many successful kingdoms, particularly the Vijayanagara Empire, the Satavahanas and the Kakatiyas. The other famous quote is attributed to Italian traveller Niccolò de' Conti who, after many years of travelling across the southern states, exclaimed that Telugu was the 'Italian of the East'. This is owed to the fact that every Telugu word 'organic' to the language ends with a vowel and that leads to the spoken word having a gentle song-like quality.

Recent history, too, paints a favourable picture of reformers' attempts to preserve and diffuse Telugu literature (original and translated works) among the masses and the marginalized. The architect of the now largely forgotten Public Library Movement in India was Iyyanki Venkata Ramanayya, who, through Herculean efforts, pushed for the establishment of libraries across all districts, *talukas* and blocks so that spaces of knowledge were available to all (including women, a revolutionary idea at that time) as early as 1919. For this, he was awarded the Padma Shri. He set up the country's first journal on library science in 1916. Other efforts were taken to translate Shakespeare, Rabindranath Tagore and classics by other writers into the vernacular so that Telugu readers could have access to them. Names like Sharat, Nirmala or the suffix 'babu' at the end of a name are the result of the influx of Bengali texts. George

Orwell personally sanctioned the translation of his classic *Animal Farm: A Fairy Story* into Telugu by Janamanchi Ramakrishna as *Pasuvuladivanam: Uhakalpitameinapeddakatha.*

And yet, despite the royal patronage and the efforts of reformists from the nineteenth and twentieth centuries, the readership of Telugu literature continues to decline. The Telugu poet Aarudra is supposed to have said, 'The oyster doesn't make the pearls / with the jeweller in mind. The poet doesn't make poems / with the reader in mind.' But surely, even he would worry a little about the reader who seems to have gone missing. The quest to make sense of this disappearance of Telugu literature from readers' hands and the increasing audience for the film writer's craft began when I was in school as I clawed through history.

Another World, Another World
Another World Beckons,
Onwards, Upwards,
Let Us Strive
To Fly Higher!
    – *Mahaprasthanam* (The Great Journey to A New World)

The Hacks Lived Happily Ever After

I learnt about the history of Telugu language through a project in school in the eighth grade. It involved chart paper, sketch pens, paper cut-outs, and peeling dried glue, while imagining it to be a substitute for skin – that's how serious I was about it.

It involved me learning and memorizing about the first set of Telugu writers-cum-poets – Nannayya, Thikkana and Yerrapragada. All one paragraph write-ups about them had a path of glitter that led to freshly printed black-and-white images of the poet from the internet. Here's what I had proudly written down on pink chart paper.

Nannayya – he was the first Telugu poet, had translated the Sanskrit Mahabharatha into Telugu. He increased the Telugu lexicon by borrowing words from the Sanskrit language. He was the first half of a trio of writers called 'kavithraya' (The Trinity of Poets). He wrote heavily in verse. He wrote the first two-and-a-half chapters. Nannaya began writing at the order of the King Raja Narendra to counter the forces of Jainism.

Thikkana – The second member of trinity, Thikkana, did not finish the incomplete chapter. Rather, he wrote the next fifteen chapters. His style was mostly in prose and for that he used more Telugu words than Sanskrit words. Thikkana was also a minister for the Kakatiya kings who tried to bridge Shaivism and Vaishnavism.

Yerrapragada – The final member of the trinity, finished the incomplete chapter left by Nannayya. While none dared to finish because they were afraid to match Nannayya's skill, Yerrapragada completed the task. A staunch Shaivite, he wrote in the court of a Reddy King.

The engine of this project was a passionate Telugu teacher who was keen on making students who loved the language in a world where it was eroding even among native Telugu speakers. *We didn't know enough. We wouldn't try hard enough before slipping in an English word in our sentences, we didn't read enough Telugu books.* All legitimate complaints. All true. A short man with white wispy hair and a French beard that was trimmed to perfection, the teacher had a perennial smile as if he was making peace with a joke at his expense. He ensured that we watched Telugu plays, took classes under a tree so that we don't feel confined to a classroom, went off script so that we were not bound by the text.

And yet, we barely showed interest in the language beyond the curriculum or the marks that we needed to secure.

After watching *Simhadri*, when I re-joined the new academic year with a new-found interest in Telugu and its history, in me he saw a protégé. It seemed to him as if years of his persistence had paid off. He was keen on developing me – in fact, anybody who would just stick to the language – as someone interested in Telugu and its literature. He finally had an ear for his complaints about how Hindi students would stage plays, while Telugu students seemed to be embarrassed by their native tongue; Hindi teachers were many, but Telugu teachers far fewer. He was careful to ensure that the tone never became resentful, just wistful words upon finding out that the grass was really greener on the Hindi side. In me he could see, after a long time, a chance at moulding a 'true student of the language' – probably after himself.

The first step was to change my handwriting. While most students of Telugu are taught to write in accordance with the script – curvy letters that match the vowel-laden language – my handwriting, in the words of my Telugu professor, looked like 'hundred drunkards leading each through a dimly lit street'. Over time, I sandpapered the jagged edges of my handwriting into rounded curves.

He then moved to preparing me for a cultural festival where students from neighbouring schools would celebrate different aspects of Telugu culture. Having been to such festivals before, my teacher was certain that other students would present on tame topics. Usually in such events, students would regurgitate facts fed to them by their teachers. *Ugadi is the Telugu new year festival. Sankranti is the spring festival.* Or, *Andhra Pradesh has twenty-eight districts. The state has two hundred and ninety-four seats. The current chief minister of Andhra Pradesh is Y.S. Rajashekhara Reddy.* Worst of all, he complained, would be the projects where students wrote about the life of a farmer in a fictitious village in one of the Telugu states. Based on broad stereotypes, students would dress up as 'farmers' and talk about the day in the life of a farmer. A supposed play, the act would end up looking more like a fancy-dress competition for schools to take adequate photos than projects where students were pushed by teachers to learn about the history of Telugu culture and literature. We were going to change that, and he was sure our project was going to be eye-catching. There was even a prize for the best presentation. He believed it was about time that 'real' students who put effort into this festival were rewarded.

After writing about the trinity of Nannayya, Thikkana and Yerrapragada, he taught me about Telugu literature's infamous brothers-in-law poets Srinatha and Pothana – the former a Hedonistic poet and the latter a devotional poet who would bow down to no king, but only the god he believed in. While Srinatha converted his writing into material currency, Pothana considered poverty honourable. Pothana worshipped God, while Srinatha was worshipped by kings.

Pothana was a poet and a farmer who was famous for his book on *Andhra Maha Bhagavatham*, the Telugu translation of the original Sanskrit poem, which focuses on the different avatars of Vishnu. Pothana's most famous work is familiar to most Telugu students – either as a poem crammed into syllabus or as a story that trickled into their life through their parents, or some element of pop-culture. Titled *Gajendra Moksham* (The Liberation of Gajendra) narrates the tale of an Elephant King who gets bitten by a crocodile in a lake. Unable to wrestle away the creature, the Elephant King prays to Lord Vishnu to help him and offers a lotus in return. The devotee's pain and cry for help is enough to shake the God from his comfortable abode in heaven and save Gajendra from the wrath of the crocodile. In contrast to Pothana, Srinatha exhibits far more flamboyance in his verse He frames his understanding of what constitutes a good poem as thus:

> *A little crooked like the crescent on Shiva's head,*
> *Sharp as the contours of the firm, quickened breasts of the Goddess*
> *Roused to fury at the end of time, yet soft and delicious,*
> *Good poetry is all of this together*
> *dancing forever wherever poets live.*

Srinatha pushes the envelope of what is sacred and the boundaries of the artform by making the ordinary unfamiliar. He was a favourite among kings because he was known to barter his poetry by dedicating his work to kings. Insecure kings found in Srinatha a poet par excellence, willing to preserve them in history. Srinatha's dependence on the royal patronage can be seen in his last poem.

Who will wine me and dine me on plates of Gold?
Bhaskara long ago met his maker.
It's hard to go on living in this dying age
Now it's time for the poets in heaven
To shake in terror, Srinatha, the Undefeated,
Is on his way.

The contrast in the popular perception of these poets can also be understood through the actors starring in the two hagiographic biopics that both the poets got. Pothana's biopic titled *Bhakta Potana* (Potana, the Devotee) had Chittoor Nagaiah as its lead. One of the first Telugu actors who jumped from on stage in theatre to in front of the camera, influenced by Gandhi and a staunch believer in Ramana Maharshi, Chittoor Nagaiah was the 'intellectual' matinee idol immersing himself in his roles, a method actor who made every emotion he felt apparent and clear to the audience. The film begins with Pothana praising Rama; the first image on-screen is a camera panning down on the statue of Rama, while Pothana sings praises akin to the shot introducing the hero.

On the other hand, in Srinatha's biopic titled *Srinatha Kavi Sarvabhoumudu* (Srinatha, the Emperor among Poets), the titular role is played by NTR. In the film, the first image on-screen is that of NTR delivering a monologue. *Before* the titles have even rolled. It's NTR walking through the set of the film as he espouses the greatness of Srinatha, emphasizing multiple times on the poet's obsession with food and poetry, and his womanizing ways. NTR seems to talk about the life that was lived by Srinatha – a rich life full of ups and downs and pleasures and pains, while he achieved artistic excellence and planted the Telugu flag in India's literary history. It's a genius meta moment where the actor playing the part could be talking about both himself and the subject of the biopic. This might seem vain, even by NTR's standards, but *Srinatha Kavi Sarvabhoumudu* was the last ever film NTR acted in, so the film and the opening monologue served as a reminder for posterity for the poet as well as the actor. Even in his own biopic, Srinatha preserved one last Hero.

My Telugu teacher and I got closer in our pursuit of understanding the history of Telugu literature, finding the role of the writer in its crevasses. While telling me about *Srinatha Kavi Sarvabhoumudu*, he revealed one more secret. This one was personal. A little beyond my years even, but maybe it was years of being a Telugu teacher to reluctant students that he needed to confess. I asked him if he liked NTR a lot because I couldn't help, but notice him smile whenever he spoke about NTR He paused as if to estimate my ability to comprehend his answer. He probably believed that it didn't matter. He had to say it.

Years earlier, in 1972, he had seen a film called *Badi Panthulu* (School Teacher), where NTR plays the titular schoolteacher. He takes charge of a school run by Paparaayudu, a corrupt president of the school committee for whom the school stands as a space from where he can swindle money. The school is in absolute disarray, so much that on his first day the students demand a holiday because it's the new teacher's first day. But this isn't a *Dead Poets Society*-esque story about a teacher who changes one batch of students in a school. This story explores the characters further. It's about Raghava Rao (NTR), whose name is a synonym for Rama, and his wife Janaki. It's about the ideals that Raghava Rao vehemently sticks to despite the poverty his job keeps pushing him into. He is heavily influenced by the idea of India espoused by Gandhi, Nehru, Tagore and Sarvepalli Radhakrishna, in whose honour the nation celebrates Teacher's Day. Their photos adorn the background walls of his house, the police station he finds himself in, the walls of the school.

Raghava Rao also believes that punishing and reprimanding students doesn't shape students into the best version of themselves; rather it's a teacher's duty to teach them the difference between right and wrong. When an errant student, Ramu, steals a pen, he tells him that he should rather use his bravery for becoming a police officer than a thief – that bravery is better used in upholding the system than cheating it. To encourage the young boy to become a police officer, Raghava Rao gifts him the pen. But this film isn't about Ramu or Raghava Rao. *Not yet, at least.* The students love him so much that when Raghava Rao's house is set on fire by Paparaayudu, and they see their teacher homeless, the students build another house through sheer determination. They struggle, but they sing too. Young boys and young girls no older than ten pick up spades, bricks, cement, and build their favourite teacher a new house. And that's what the film is about. *The house.* It isn't just a house to Raghava Rao. It's made of bricks, cement, and the idea of India espoused by Nehru, Tagore, Gandhi and Sarevepalli Radhakrisha. It's a bloody monument to the values he believes in.

The film's antagonists, Paparaayudu and fate, try to snatch the home away from Raghava Rao. At some point, when he is forced to pay dowry to the in-laws of his daughter, he even falls at the feet of his to-be brother-in-law. My teacher laughed, while telling me about this moment because as young fans of NTR, they all collectively gasped. Not at the flagrant disregard for the anti-dowry laws the in-law had displayed. But because NTR, who had played god in his previous films, fell at the feet of another actor. But the scene worked. Because if NTR fell at someone's feet, then Raghava Rao was really desperate. He agrees to pay-off the dowry in small instalments, but also mortgages the house, in case he is unable to pay. It breaks the man. But he has to do what he has to. The man, who taught progressive values to his students all his life, is broken by the same dogma he tried to fight.

Yet, his two sons and daughter barely see the importance of the house. One of the sons is played by another Hero, Krishnam Raju, who would later go on to become a star and a member of parliament from Kakinada. The college educated sons grow up wayward in their pursuit of material wealth – something they never had. In this pursuit of happiness, they compromise in their ethics by tolerating their dubious in-laws. Raghava Rao's son-in-law is not evil, but incompetent. He admits that he is not educated like Raghava Rao's sons and therefore he can't stop his own father from hounding after the dowry. As Raghava Rao is unable to pay-off his debts, he is forced out of his house and the house is auctioned away to the highest bidder. Defeated and broken, Raghava Rao has nothing to prove for his service to the nation and no family, but his wife.

Badi Panthulu borrows from the Hollywood film *Make Way for Tomorrow*, in which the children, unable to share the economic burden of the parents together, decide to split them across two houses. Similarly, against their wishes, Raghava Rao and his wife are split between the two sons. It's a metaphor the country abandoning its values and treating them like a burden. NTR – so often the dashing hero, the man who played God on-screen, the charmer who sings songs under the moonlight – suddenly seems so old, fragile and vulnerable. He is ably supported by Anjali Devi, who plays his wife, Janaki.

Janaki is treated like a maid in the house of the first son. In the second son's house, Raghava Rao is constantly humiliated for his age, disease, failing eyes, and the last straw is when he is accused of stealing a pearl necklace. Raghava Rao is even arrested and taken to the police station. The man who promised to build a better country is thrown in jail. *Almost.* Because the police officer in charge of the station is none other than Ramu, the student who had once been a thief. He knows that his teacher could have done no wrong.

That's the moment. The million-dollar moment in the theatre when a young man who adored NTR and sported a thick black French beard had decided to become a teacher. Specifically, a Telugu teacher. When Raghava Rao's own sons had deserted him and doubted him, the students he had taught honoured his words. My Telugu teacher had made that fateful decision just when Ramu tells Raghava he has become a police officer following the words of his teacher. It is then revealed that Ramu was the one who bought the house for Raghava Rao, who is made to sign on paper that he will never leave the house.

Except, Raghava Rao doesn't have a pen. He's not a teacher anymore. Just a frail old man, who's been treated like a burden by his family. And then Ramu gives his teacher the very pen he had once received. The moment that changes his life. When Raghava Rao signs with the pen that he had once given as a gift, my teacher had imagined a million memorable moments with his future students. But teaching Telugu hadn't really attracted too many students. Not only were the number of students dwindling in his experience, but they also lacked interest. And even those interested were only in it for the marks.

To him, the cultural festival was the moment where he could live out the fantasy that NTR had drafted for him in *Badi Panthulu*. An interested student. And his near-infinite wisdom. There was no house. There was no Ramu. His children were great people who would take care of him. But it felt as though if enough effort was put into the project and we won the prize, he would have that moment again. The moment he had when he saw *Badi Panthulu* in 1972.

After finishing Srinatha and Pothana, we jumped a few centuries to the first modern great poet of Telugu literature Gurujada Apparao. He enjoyed the patronage of the King of Vizianagaram in the nineteenth century and was a progressive writer. His most popular work *Kanyasulkam* (Brides for Sale) is a critique of Brahminical puritanism by focusing on clean and the 'unclean' and the idea of child marriage and widow remarriage. Its greatest trick is in its protagonists, Gireesam, and Madhuravani, and Pootakoola Munda (the widow who owns a local food court). Gireesam is an English-educated seemingly progressive Brahmin, whose words ring empty as his actions enable the system as much as the staunch conservative Brahmin figures that surround him. Madhuravani, on the other hand, is a prostitute and is 'unclean', but walks the moral tightrope more ably than Gireesam. And Pootakoola Munda is a young widow, whom society abandons after pushing her into a marriage where she is sold to an old man for cash. Through these characters, Gurajada Apparao chews away at the times he lives in, hoping to spit out a more equitable progressive future. My teacher was quick to point out that there is even an NTR film where he played Gireesam in the cinema adaptation of *Kanyasulkam*. But this time he doesn't digress as much.

Even in Apparao's popular poem *Desamunu Preminchamanna* (Love the Country) the most popular lines are hidden in its stanzas.

> A country doesn't amount to its soil
> A country amounts to its people.

But my teacher pointed out that equally important and more reflective of his progressive values are the lines:

> What use is it looking back
> When history has such little good?

We decided that these six poets were good representations of Telugu literary history and the place they occupied at their respective times. The project was ready. Pink chart paper, glitter, images glued to the paper. A timeline that placed each writer in their respective century. We had rehearsed my presentation. Like a meal with starters, I would first speak about Nanniah, Thikkana and Yerrapragada and their unique styles in translating the Mahabharatha. Then I would move to the contrasting lives of the poets Pothana and Srinatha – the courtier poet and the farmer poet. And as dessert, I would end with the importance of Gurajada Apparao to modern Telugu students.

I was confident. My Telugu teacher was happy. We set out for the festival.

Once there, the usual suspects were present. There was a presentation on the basic political makeup of then united Andhra Pradesh. There was also one about Ugadi and Sankranti – the Telugu festivals. And worst of all, there were the students who were pretending to be farmers from a fictional village called Ramapuram. My Telugu teacher derided his hacky counterparts on their lack of effort put into students. He was praising me, but he was clearly praising himself.

The cultural festival itself was a chaotic affair with hundreds of students and scores of teachers trying to tame the students. Cramped stalls no bigger than railway compartments were given to student-teacher duos to put up their projects. Adding to the crowd were parents who had come to take photos of the event with bright flashes, while directing their awkward children to look towards the lens of the camera. My parents couldn't come, but what disappointed me more was that pink chart paper was a common choice for presenting information. My teacher consoled me by pointing out that my content was probably stronger than the others. Each visitor at our stall was impressed with the information that was available. Parents of other children, particularly the fathers, were impressed by the names rolling out of my mouth; they would occasionally grunt in appreciation. The appreciative handshakes poured in both to my teacher and me.

Except, each parent would tell us that there was a similar stall at the other end of the festival. At first, in mild arrogance, we laughed it off. We were sure we had nailed our presentation, which covered over five hundred years of history. But as the number of visitors who spoke about our apparent counterparts grew, we were determined to estimate the 'other' stall. My teacher, like an antique collector who finds out that a precious diamond was fake, first went to inspect the other stall. In the few minutes he disappeared, I struggled to muster confidence in my presentation. I was stuttering for the first time. Then my teacher returned, disappointed.

Something was rotten in the cultural festival.

I continued to present to other visitors, but my teacher was lost in thought. A few minutes later, a young boy who was my age and size accompanied by an older man, much larger in size with a newly dyed misplaced black moustache, wearing thick-rimmed brown spectacles and thinning hair, visited the stall. The boy looked terrified, as if he had been forced to accept a crime he did not commit. My teacher too walked and stood next to me. It felt like being in the middle of a Mexican stand-off, with the students acting as the malfunctioning guns.

I began my presentation by pointing out to the pink chart paper. *Nannayya. Thikkana. Yerrapragada. Mahabharata.* Words rehearsed over many days, which felt like ghee on my tongue, suddenly seemed to drag my tongue out of my mouth to the floor with their sheer weight. By the time I reached my point about the respective styles of writing of the poets, I was interrupted.

'What you're saying is incomplete. Praveen, why don't you talk about Nannayya, Thikkana, Yerrapragada. You know better.' Praveen, the young boy, began to talk.

'Nannayya, considered the first writer, had also destroyed the texts of Jain and Buddhist monks before him. He was working in the –'

'Sir. First, let my student complete.' My teacher butted in. Like hot coffee after a spicy breakfast, words sizzled out of his mouth. Because of this rude interruption, all the words in my mouth had pushed themselves into my head and were dying to make an exit. My prepubescent Adam's apple too kept trying to tear a hole and escape through my throat. It didn't help that a small crowd of parents had gathered to watch the two teachers compete, like it was a fight between two roosters.

I began anyway. I jumped through history straight towards Pothana and Srinatha. Brothers-in-law. Gods. Kings. Contrast. Duality.

'Sir, they were actually not brothers-in-law. That is just a myth. What kind of nonsense is your student talking?' Even Praveen began to give me sympathetic looks.

'Sir, mind your tongue.' My teacher said. 'He's a student.'

'Well, your student clearly has wrong teachers. Pothana wasn't just about god. Srinatha wasn't just about kings. Looks like someone just saw films and came here.'

Maybe because it was partially true, my teacher moved forward to draw the sword of Telugu literary history. He was not ready to lose face. He was not going to let some stranger steal his *Badi Panthulu* moment. 'I heard your student talk about Krishna Deva Raya. Is someone worthy of a poet only if they are a king?'

'Oh, if someone is really worried about the speaking for the oppressed, why isn't your student talking about Sri Sri? Why haven't you taught your student about Volga? Why isn't your student wearing a loin cloth and singing like Gaddar?' Sri Sri was a leftist poet who also worked in cinema. Volga is the pen name of Telugu feminist author P. Lalita Kumari, who at one point worked in the studio division of Usha Kiran films. Gaddar is a revolutionary poet and balladeer who worked for the cause of a separate Telangana. He won a state award as the Best Playback Singer for a film titled *Jai Bolo Telangana*.

Soon, the issue escalated and lost civility and both men lost their tempers. At first, the battlefield was Telugu literary history. Next, it became the students they had taken under their wing. And after that it became each other's mothers. Others intervened and chided both the men for adding a sour taste to the cultural festival. The two teams were sent to their respective stalls. The crowd thinned out at both the respective stalls; eventually, nobody wanted to come to our cursed sites, which apparently presented skewed literary history. My teacher continued to hammer into me how the other teacher was wrong. *He is expecting too much from young students. He first abused me when I spoke about literature. He thinks he's intelligent only because he wears glasses, that goat-brained idiot.*

Within a few hours, the argument, much like the writers they were arguing for, seemed centuries ago. Except for the two of us, nobody else seemed to remember it. At some point, Praveen and his teacher, like a breath, exited the festival without anybody noticing. When we were wrapping up, like our mood, the pink chart paper had dampened and its corners curled inwards. The photos I stuck to the paper clung to it like mountaineers on jagged rocks. My teacher maintained a distance between us as we headed back.

The prize eventually went to the farmer from the village of Ramapuram. The pictures of the event even made it to the local district edition of a daily newspaper. The 'farmer', his teacher, his parents, all posed for a happy picture.

> And what shall their tired eyes see?
> A fallen dream,
> A removed heaven!
> And what do their scattered hearts feel?
> There, here
> An advancing doom!
>
>   – *Parajithulu* (The Defeated)

Hyderabad – Home of Heroes

Most Telugu intellectuals who made their way into cinema were relegated to roles where they became ornament to Heroes. Gollapudi Maruthi Rao, whose plays have been part of curriculum for students of Masters in Telugu, was permanently reduced to a supporting artist. His work only reduced in its importance to the 'scripts' that Telugu heroes demanded. It is ironic that one of Maruthi Rao's last few memorable roles in cinema was in the film *Leader* (Leader), starring Rana Daggubati released in 2010 and the debut film of the Baahubali actor. In it, Arjun Prasad, a young political Chief Minister and the son of a former CM played by Rana, the scion of Suresh

Productions and a third-generation member of the film fraternity and a second-generation actor, lectures the character played by Rao, a corrupt and aged politician that it is better he dies than corrupt the Andhra Legislative Assembly. L.B. Sriram, another such excellent actor reduced to playing supporting roles, and a star thespian who has contributed to Telugu theatre, has been reduced to playing characters whose roles have barely any importance or has been side-lined to play characters who praise the Hero. Brahmanandam, Telugu cinema's most well-known comic personality, has a Master's in Telugu, and has been playing a comedian often becoming tamed by Hero if not fooled by them.

But the decline in respect for the practitioners of the language and the trend of Hero-worship has one more crucial factor. Unlike literature, cinema can be distributed easily to even the illiterate masses of a society. This is a problem innate to all societies which have massive film industries, whose awesome financial power can bulldoze through any obstructions. The Telugu film industry is a curious one, because for the longest time even after the formation of a separate state (then Andhra Pradesh), its central node remained Chennai till as late as the '90s.

Maybe it was the feeling of having overstayed their welcome. Or that a separate Telugu state had existed for long enough. Or maybe the film personalities got tired of the exhausting plane journeys and missed the stardom their Tamil peers enjoyed in Chennai.

At first, they trickled out of Chennai to Hyderabad, and then, only once it found patrons such as Ramoji Rao and A. Nageshwar Rao, like a pricked water balloon did it completely spill out. This meant that the industry had to build itself twice and the second time – when it shifted to Hyderabad it depended on these very patrons who built studios. ANR built Annapoorna Studios; Ramoji Rao, whose news daily *Eenadu* became a mouthpiece for NTR, built the Ramoji Film City; Ramanaidu, the producer, built Ramanaidu Studios and was known for his close ties with NTR; Chiranjeevi with the help of his brother-in-law Allu Arvind set up Geeta Arts. ANR moved in '70s and was adamant that he would act in films if, and only if, they were produced in Andhra Pradesh, making exceptions for big studios like Vahini and Venus Studio. The new centre of Telugu cinema was constructed in Hyderabad. Unlike the organic growth it saw in Chennai, it could only survive by large investments by producer oligarchs who for obvious reasons cemented their own interests.

The power of the stars turned out to be a double-edged sword for writers. Once NTR became a superstar of mythic proportions, writers had to bend to his demands to maintain his image. With NTR's political role, his power became even more daunting. While Tamil Nadu, Andhra Pradesh and Karnataka have a very strong culture of film-star-politicians, what sets NTR apart from M.G. Ramachandran (M.G.R.), another superstar-turned chief minister is that, while M.G.R. walked into existing political parties with a strong sense of Tamil identity, NTR brought about a sense of Telugu identity into the public sphere, including the disinterested masses and middle class. Even the characters played by both of them were significantly different – M.G.R. often played the common man who struggled for the upliftment of his fellow men, while NTR played Hindu deities.

Once NTR became chief minister of the state, he was forever etched into the public imagination as a saviour; more importantly, he set a benchmark for actors who wanted to achieve mega stardom. Thus, the films of the '90s played to the new aspirations of actors, as well as expectations from an audience that now expected demigods. This left little room for literature in a field dominated by mythic god-like actors. In the '90s, yet another Telugu superstar, Chiranjeevi, tried to emulate the footsteps of NTR in politics, and though he failed, the footsteps continue to be the same.

In any nation's history
Where is the reason for Pride?

All human history
Is Man Against Man, in search of Glory.
All human history
Is Man oppressing Man;
All human history
Is written in blood on fields of war.

—*Desacharithralu* (Histories of Nations)

The Language of Literature

One can argue that states such as Tamil Nadu and Kerala, which too have flourishing film industries with aged superstars that dictate scripts, still have thriving literary circuits. But one needs to understand the history of Andhra Pradesh as a political project. The then Andhra Pradesh was a state carved out of the Madras Presidency in 1953, after Potti Sreeramulu fasted unto death in Madras. The capital was shifted from Kurnool to the once Nizam-controlled territory of Hyderabad. This meant that the centres of power had shifted from the Telugu-speaking zone of Kurnool to a newly created vacuum in Hyderabad. So, the new state was forced into social cohesion with an administrative capital in Hyderabad, an old-school capital in Kurnool, and literary powerhouses distributed across Vishakhapatnam, Vijayawada and Chennai (then Madras).

Andhra Pradesh was forcefully fit together, deepening the distrust between Telangana, and the coastal and interior regions of the new state. The Telugu literature produced during this period stagnated at upper-caste levels. A particular caste-based literary conflict that remains unresolved is the 'language' that qualifies as literature itself. The distinction between colloquial and formal literary language is sharp, with the latter marked by stylized grammar, complicated structuring and a heavy dosage of Sanskritization that is indicative of upper-caste roots. As the colloquial language evolved, 'high literature' failed to stay contemporaneous. This generated a tug-of-war of sorts between the purists and the 'philistines' who used simpler grammar and texture to express stories, but whose language was not considered 'literary' by critics and connoisseurs. The Telugu Hero, unlike the 'high literature' protagonists, spoke a language that could be heard in everyday conversation and the Telugu film writers added words to everyday lexicon. This does not mean that their problems were representative of everyday struggles of the Telugu society, but just that they spoke a language that was easily accessible en masse.

Moreover, the state's civil space has been divided amongst competing identities, which includes revolutionary literature from the Naxal movement of the '80s, the rise of the Dalit protagonists after that, and now the rise of progressive feminist voices through Volga. Unlike other states where Dalit writers like Paul Chirakkarode of Kerala and feminist Dalit voices like Bama from Tamil Nadu found recognition and readers, these writers were restricted to their politics and did not find mass readership. And more recently, directors like Pa. Ranjith managed to convince the superstar of India, Rajnikanth, to act in *Kabali and Kaala*, films with a clear Dalit protagonist. Dalit – and other political – literature produced in Telugu has, instead, been reduced to political activism through movements, such as the Madiga Dandora movement, which aimed to unify the Madiga caste (the lowest amongst the caste hierarchies). Writer-poets/balladeers such as Gaddar occupy a space in the popular imagination as producers of literature and songs for only specific emancipatory purposes and solidify the idea that songs written in the local tongue do not qualify as 'literature'. In the public sphere of literature consumption, this means that literature by such lower-caste writers is meant for certain reader groups only and that these stories will not find publishing space or larger acceptance. Leading Telugu publishing houses have stayed away from publishing 'activist' literature, and this kind of work is also neglected by 'average' readers.

The liberalization of the early '90s and the creation of Hyderabad as an IT hub by the government of Chandrababu Naidu also had an impact. An excessive obsession with software engineers who could emigrate to the US meant that people with access to literature and literature capital escaped the state, while the voices that wanted to be heard were left unpublished and relegated to the margins. The other social impact of this 'dream' is the IITs and IIT coaching centres with toxic educational conditions for teenagers that have emerged amidst universal demand across the state. A new trend that has emerged in Telangana is the denouncement of classical Andhra writers to make room for Telangana writers. The political sphere has posited the two as mutually exclusive options, thus justifying the move to eliminate Andhra writers from the state's syllabi. This has extended to other subjects such as social studies and geography and has been done with encouragement from the Telangana Education Minister G. Jagadish Reddy and Chief Minister K. Chandrashekhar Rao.

A soft ray of hope in all the bleakness is that the non-residential Indian (NRI) Telugu population has been very active in retaining and encouraging the Telugu culture – be it in the form of dance, music or the written word. The alienation and disconnect from US pop-culture probably prompts the diaspora to cling to their language. It is ironic to hear Telugu being freely spoken on the streets of Dallas and San Francisco, whereas children in the schools of Hyderabad stutter and struggle through basic comprehension passages. This partial revival of the Telugu 'culture' through the NRI community also opens up the question of who defines and owns this culture. The demographics of the Telugu diaspora are representative of the caste structure prevalent in the Telugu-speaking states. The upper-caste bias in that demographic and the quasi-Brahminical tones of the definitions of 'culture' continue to be exclusionary and elitist, thus abetting the current crisis.

After my complicated journey to find the causes of the problem, I found myself on the phone with current Telugu author Chandralatha who is on a Quioxtic mission to 'educate' readers through small posts on social media. By using the medium, she manages to connect to potential readers across the globe but, literally, on her own terms. By using small poems, haikus or paragraphs, she urges all the Telugu authors to connect to readers in such a manner. Of course, the internet as a means to read literature is yet to become a truly mass phenomenon in the Telugu-speaking states, but somewhere in that attempt seems to lie an approach that has not been tried in all these decades of decline.

> For work, for food,
> To work in a city,
> The traveller left,
> Not heeding to their mother's advice
> They walked for three days not knowing their way…
> —*Baatasaari* (The Traveller)

Reader versus Audience

Each generation constructs and reconstructs its idea of culture based on what it receives from the previous generations. It is necessary to understand the dominant media, language and identities of the current generation and zeitgeist in the culture-making process. Be it cinema, social media, the spoken language or the voices of those at the margins – these are all aspects of current society that need to be involved in the process of producing literature. Inclusion needs to be the order of the day, shying away from these different aspects of culture and locking up the Telugu literature in self-constructed notions of purity and nostalgia won't do.

The Telugu literature's '*mahaprasthnam*' or great journey to a new world is a path made of rough terrain that has cinema, caste, politics of state, the nostalgic NRI and the hitherto unknown beast that is social media. Literature lies dormant and unable to reach its reader. The book and the word seem to be slipping away from the hands of the reader. But here, the guiding light can be found no further than the book on my table – *Mahaprasthnam*, in which Sri Sri exclaims:

A pup, a matchstick, a bar of soap –
Don't look down on anything!
Everything is worthy of poetry!

4

Badly Cast(E) Heroes: The Missing Case of Red Cinema and People's Star

'I know now that doors open as quickly as they close. That nothing very good or very bad lasts for very long.'

—Shehan Karunatilaka, Chinaman:
The Legend of Pradeep Mathew

A Badly Cast(e) Hero

The Telugu Heroes are useful creatures. They can transport the audience into another world, making them wonder if these on-screen individuals are made of the same bones as ordinary humans. These Heroes can fight and show audience the thin line between right and wrong. They can take people who can never afford a flight ticket to Paris and tell them it's the city of romance. They assure the viewers that questioning the system is valid – that doctors can be evil, lawyers can be corrupt and that farmers are suffering.

But once their make-up is washed away, their wigs removed, and like their hairlines, they eventually recede in the public memory,

Heroes *can* enter politics. And even though they enter as Heroes, they inevitably end up as politicians – because as much as cinema screens convince us otherwise, heroes are human too. *Indian humans.* And like all Indian humans, they belong to a 'caste'. And when push comes to vote, they use this caste, and other castes that support their caste, to place themselves in positions of power. Even if they are reluctant to use and own their caste, the caste catches up because a Hero is forged on-screen and brought together by the love of the people.

In post-Independence Andhra, it has been difficult to create pan-caste figures that are loved by all groups. When the country was fighting the British, it was easy to identify the villain. Pale skin, funny accents, racist, and all-round oppressor of the Indian people. But it's not so easy to identify villains in a post-colonial world. They have come from within 'us'. As governments and people look to replace the 'outsiders' with new ones we are not sure any more what it means to be 'Indian' without an enemy to hate. Perhaps the struggle for independence gave Indians a simplistic conceptualization of villains. These villains made it easier to spot our Heroes, and the worse the villain got, the bigger our Heroes became. But after Independence, our stories became more complex. Enemies sometimes became friends and then became enemies again. Heroes became villains became heroes. Yet, cinema screens continued to deliver easily identifiable heroes and villains – despite the changing times.

It was at this juncture that the wolfish eyes of 'caste' swooped in and gobbled the Telugu Hero to forward its ends. The big 'C' word that dominates India and its politics. The Telugu Heroes have beaten many bad guys, but even they've proven to be too small to take on this plague. When they couldn't beat them, they decided to join them.

To understand how the Telugu Heroes are tied to caste, let us look at the story of the one Hero who tried to take on the system. To some people, he tried and failed; to some, that he tried is itself a success; and according to him, he's going to keep trying. While every caste and every Telugu Hero tried to forward their own interests, with results ranging from astounding success to utter debacles, one Hero stood out – the hero once called *People's Star*. This Hero tried to take on the caste system from 'underneath' and challenged those on top for nearly two decades in the '80s and '90s.

But he's struggling now. He is still around. He still makes films like he always has. He even makes sure he never plays supporting characters, as ageing actors often do. He is still 'The Hero'. Even his films haven't changed much: their themes may have changed, but the spirit remains the same. In terms of cinema and metaphor, the Hero – and the genre that became popular with him – have died a slow painful death. But who killed him? Who killed the genre that made him popular? Because the death is metaphorical, the suspects must be abstract entities – like castes, political parties and economic interests.

The death of *People's Star* is not a classic mystery with clean answers and clear motivations, as nothing is when it comes to the issue of caste in India. I am neither Sherlock Holmes nor Miss Marple, but there is indeed an element of whodunnit to the metaphorical death of *People's Star*.

The Detective and His Sidekick: Blue Films and Red Armies

I met *People's Star* in a place where 'decent' people don't ordinarily go. It was in a theatre where they played 'blue films'.

I was very young when I understood what a *blue film* was. Dangerously young. I tell people I was twelve years old.

That's a lie. I was seven. But in my pursuit of the blue film, I also saw my first film that spoke about caste and exploitation of Adivasi tribes in what is now Telangana and parts of Northern Andhra. I learnt about the Naxal movement and the way it gripped the Telugu states. It was the first time I learnt about R. Narayana Murthy – *People's Star*.

The 'blue' film adventure began because the school bus we took journeyed through the longest route before dropping all the children home. Mine was the last stop, which meant that I got to see a tour of the full town of Anantapur – its narrow roads, open drains that had plastic covers floating like aimless boats on black rivers, the luscious smell of fried batter and fresh coffee that every food stall and household exhumed to drown the smell of a hard day's sweat and exhaust. I befriended a boy who was known only by his initials, DK His stop was the last before mine. He was scrawny, with a perennially terrible haircut and an extra finger, an inhaler always jutting out of his fist because of his asthma. The red dust of Anantapur and the buses with ancient diesel combustion engines that released thick, black smoke waged a constant war against DK's respiratory system. He would win most times, but occasionally, his coughing fits would irritate other students because of which he had taken to sitting on the last seat with me. Our friendship blossomed over these bus rides to and from school.

DK had an elder sister, whom he hated. He loved films of Pawan Kalyan, then a rising star. He wanted to become a boxer one day, like Kalyan did in the film *Thammudu* (Younger Brother). According to DK, once he grew up, his asthma would disappear and the first person he would box would be his sister.

I divulged secrets too. I hated the food my grandmother made. It was too spicy. There was a girl called Cherry in my class who I loved – the kind of love that the Telugu heroes promised the Telugu heroines. (Cherry's real name was Geetha, but she became 'Cherry' because her fair cheeks were always flush with blood – like a Hollywood star's.) DK asked me if I would one day marry her. I told him only if our parents agreed to the marriage.

'And if they don't?' he asked.

'Well, then I would have to depend on my boxer friend to let his muscles do the talking.' It strengthened DK's resolve.

As children newly introduced to the Telugu cinema and its Heroes, we would also use our commute to discuss them. *Did you see Chiranjeevi dance in that film? The way Pawan Kalyan punched in that film and that guy went flying. Do you think Di Caprio in* Titanic *tried to copy Chiranjeevi's acting?*

Our conversations covered the breadth of cinema, love, family and DK's inhaler. But there was one issue we never spoke about. Between the third-last stop and DK's stop, the bus would drive past a wall adorned with posters of the Telugu cinema. At this point, all the other students would already have been dropped off, leaving the bus quite vacant: a driver at the mouth of the bus, a long empty bus like a dry tree, and two students with heavy rectangular school bags in the last seat. DK and I would stare at the wall in awkward silence, and after the bus drove about a hundred metres past it, we would resume our conversation. The wall was special because of the kind of film posters that were pasted on it. They weren't posters of 'regular' films – otherwise they would have garnished our conversations. These were different.

They were posters of the Telugu soft-porn films – 'blue' films.

The films on the posters had titles like *Stree* (Woman), *Gadilo Chappudu* (Noise from the Room), or they were posters of dubbed Shakeela films – the Malayalam actor who forayed and pioneered the boom of soft-porn films, much to the chagrin of mainstream superstars like Mohanlal and Mammootty. The images on the posters usually had a man resting his face in the bosom of a woman, a depiction that hinted at the male protagonist being confused between two women, but his wry smile said that in an ideal world, he would have them both. That theatre was the 'ideal' world. Even the theatre that played these films was called 'Neelam', meaning blue.

Every day, the bus would drive past the wall. With pinpoint precision, DK and I would pause our conversation; stare at the posters of semi-clad men and women; and hundred metres later, resume where we left off, until DK's stop arrived. The posters would change once every two or three days, reflecting the thirst of the town's young heterosexual men.

For the longest time, we never addressed 'the wall'.

Until one day we did – DK did.

'Have you ever seen those films?'

'Are you mad? If you watch *those* films, you go blind,' I replied.

DK went silent, as though betrayed for having been shamed for the first time in our conversations. I felt guilty when, hundred meters later, the conversation didn't resume because it had been irrevocably infected by silence.

'I once saw a ticket stub from Neelam theatre. It was in my uncle's back pocket. He asked me to take money from his pocket. I put the ticket back and took the money,' I said, trying to diffuse the awkwardness.

'Is he blind?'

I shook my head. My uncle had fully functioning eyes. DK smiled and started puffing from his inhaler as if he had got divine permission.

We devised a plan. The morning before we reached school, I would inform at home that I would be spending the evening in DK's house. And he would do the same in his house. Our alibi – at first it was 'studying', but knowing that we would get caught in the lie, we settled on telling family that we were playing video games in each other's houses. We would go to Neelam, buy two tickets on the spot for the evening show, and sit in the last row – lest my uncle visited again. We would watch whichever film was playing and run back home by dinner time.

The excitement was uncontrollable – so much so that I didn't even notice Cherry the whole day at school. DK and I convened in the school bus. When we reached the wall, there was an unusual poster – a hibiscus-red print, featuring an angry man wearing a green outfit and a red cloth around his neck, holding up a rifle. His face was round, eyes popping out of their sockets because of the sheer pressure the anger put on them – like an amalgamation of Che Guevara and NTR. We didn't manage to read the title, because the man on the poster was so mystifying.

When we reached DK's stop, we tip-toed to the mouth of the bus together, carrying the weight of our bags and our adventure. The bus driver gave us a puzzled look, but didn't say anything. He was probably glad that we had reduced the time he took to reach home. After we stepped down, the bus let out a celebratory puff of black smoke, which caused DK to resort to his inhaler. We walked towards Neelam in silence, making sure that we weren't caught by a familiar adult.

The world's gaze seemed to be directed at us, even the satellites in space monitoring our movements. It felt as if our families were watching us on-screens, praying to god that we wouldn't embarrass them in front of the world. They looked at the screens disappointed and angry – brandishing ladles, rolling pins, belts – as though this was a moral test that we were failing. Once we entered Neelam, they would punish us for erring.

When we reached the dilapidated single-screen theatre, it looked deserted. We finally read the title of the film for the first time: *Erra Sainyam* (The Red Army). Same angry man. This time, he had a towel wrapped around his head. Still no women.

DK dragged me by the arm before I got too fixated on the poster.

Men were packed inside Neelam, their plump Bajaj Chetak bikes and wiry TVS Lunas parked outside. Other things of note at this fine establishment were a man urinating on the outer walls of the theatre and a group of men smoking bidis.

We walked to the ticket counter, where a young man was hiding behind iron grills – his blossoming moustache wreathing his upper lip. He told us we wouldn't understand this film. We insisted on tickets. He told us, 'This is an old film that's been re-released.' We were adamant to stay. He relented and gave us two tickets made of cheap pink paper.

That we were allowed inside should have been the first sign that this film was not what we were expecting. But with lust and our sense of adventure intact, we entered the hall and took two ageing wooden chairs in the last row, making sure we were visible to nobody. The hall smelt of sweat, smoke and alcohol – the last being an unfamiliar scent back then. Men were scattered across the hall – lone warriors, and in groups of two and three.

Then the film began.

The title appeared in blinding red: *Erra Sainyam*. The credits rolled like in a news report: black screen, yellow font, news channel music.

This was the second sign that this was not the film we were expecting.

DK was extremely confused, but seemed resolved to sit through it, as if he could mentally will a blue film to appear on-screen. But it wasn't to be. The man from the poster was dancing and singing about the forest he was from. Then someone from the audience whistled and hooted and clapped. I was used to whistles and hoots in single-screen theatres, but to experience it without adult supervision terrified us. Maybe it was the *bidi* smoke getting stronger, or just panic and habit, but DK soon had the inhaler in his mouth.

On-screen, a young Adivasi woman, who is studying in a government hostel, is raped by her upper-caste warden, and she becomes pregnant. Her angry brother is on his way to beat up the warden, when the latter's brother – an aspiring MLA – intervenes by promising that the warden will marry the young woman. The brother celebrates; meanwhile, the MLA has his own scheming plans – to snatch away the land from the Adivasi man.

Suddenly, we heard the sound of a bottle being smashed against the hard-concrete floor – not on-screen, but inside Neelam theatre. DK and I grabbed each other's arms. Two men, few rows and columns away, had begun to yell abuses in Telugu – words so horrible that we were forbidden to hear them, let alone use them. It involved mothers and sisters, as these insults usually do.

On-screen, the man's land has been snatched away from him by his sister's cruel in-laws. They had even planned a second marriage for the warden – this time with a 'caste-appropriate' girl. There was something terrifying about this villainous brother-duo. These guys weren't muscular, or gruesome; they looked like real people, like they could be anyone on the street. That was the terrifying part. And the hero didn't look like a hero. The young woman looked vulnerable. DK and I were on the edge of our seats. Our plan to watch a blue film had failed miserably, and we were witnessing the worst of human behaviour on-screen and around us.

At that point, someone entered from the side doors of the theatre with a torchlight, the harsh light looking for its prey. It could have been us. It even hovered above our heads grazing our hair tips. Before it could come back a second time, we ran out of Neelam, leaving behind the pink ticket stubs, the drunkards of Anantapur, and the last two hours of *Erra Sainyam*.

We ran back to our houses as fast as we could, barely exchanging a word on the way. In the next few months, DK would change cities due to his health; and in the next year, I too would forever leave behind Neelam theatre. But I carried *Erra Sainyam* with me, hoping to finish the film one day.

I would only gather the courage to re-watch the film nearly fifteen years later, sitting in the safe confines of my house, with no alcoholics or asthmatic friends around. By then, I was also old enough to digest the plot of the film. And it struck me then that there weren't too many films like this out there.

The Crime: Nobody Killed R. Narayana Murthy

Erra Sainyam's creator and Hero, R. Narayana Murthy, is like no other in the Telugu film industry. Unlike other Heroes, he's never been in active politics, but has been courted by all the major parties in the Telugu states, including Chandrababu Naidu's TDP, the Congress and Chiranjeevi's Praja Rajyam Party (PRP). He's rejected all the offers because cinema is his passion, particularly the kind that speaks about protest.

Although he wasn't the first Hero in the genre, Narayana Murthy has become the face of a genre of cinema that is peculiar to the Telugu cinema – Erra cinema, or Red cinema. These are films whose stories have protagonists from historically oppressed castes – Dalit women, Adivasi men -who have stood helpless in the face of the atrocities committed by upper-caste men. These evil men grabbed land from the oppressed castes by making them sign on blank documents; abducting women from the oppressed caste and molesting, if not raping, them. The men and women from the oppressed castes were treated like animals, or worse, on the fields that had once been their own. They were either unpaid or paid paltry money, and their children and subsequent generations were forced into the same cycle of atrocity.

The protagonists of Erra cinema usually witness some combination of these atrocities, if not all of them. But these images don't strike as particularly new; versions of these have been seen in earlier cinema too – the Bachchan cinema for Hindi film lovers; M.G.R. cinema for Tamil film audience; even Chiranjeevi in his smash hit *Khaidi* (Prisoner), where he plays an educated poor man harassed by the village zamindar. In one sequence, when Chiranjeevi can't afford a bull to plough the field, he ties himself to the plough. His oppression renders him not just a pitiful farmer, but a beast – all his education reduced to dust and a bruised back.

So what is different about Erra cinema? It's that the protagonists of Erra cinema are clearly aware of their caste. The society around them never lets them forget it, and what makes the upper-caste men that surround the protagonists crueller than villains in other cinema is the abandon with which they use the ugly arms of the caste system. The protagonist isn't allowed to touch the villain; oppressed-caste women are constantly vulnerable to assault; the caste of the protagonist is used as an insult, yet the members of that caste are made to work on lands; if they belong to tribal castes, they are mocked for their 'strange' practices, but the upper-caste men want to steal the very forests that the tribes inhabit. Whether it contains timber, agricultural wealth or precious minerals, the site of contention is always either farmland or jungles; in other words – land.

Chiranjeevi's character in *Khaidi* was just an exploited poor villager, while Amitabh Bachchan (and countless other 'Angry Young Men' on the Indian silver screens) were angry against the rampant corruption in the system.

In contrast, the protagonists of Erra cinema are angry because they are from an oppressed caste, and there seems to be no escape for them. *No escape* – that is the other key component of Erra cinema. Just when the protagonist begins to feel clueless, there is a saviour who comes calling from the forest. Either a madman leads the protagonist to the answer or an educated person who has been disillusioned. Both appear equally mad to the protagonist. Whoever the messenger maybe, the message is the same – the forest has the answer. It's symbolic. The very forest that so many of the oppressed castes depend on – particularly the tribes in Andhra Pradesh – is being stolen from underneath their feet. The land that is being taken away from them has the answer. It has sticks, stones, bows, arrows, guns ... but more importantly, it has ideology.

What is the answer?

Naxalism, Left-leaning ideology, and some variant of the left parties. The answer contains some version of the works of Karl Marx, Vladimir Lenin and Mao Zedong; uniforms, red flags, guns, bows and arrows. The answer is in instilling fear in the upper-caste men, who have been terrorizing the innocent villagers. The answer contains violence, but it also contains freedom; it is the only resort to free oneself from oppression. So while the answer may lead to death, at least it holds a hope for escape – the possibility of reclaiming land.

In Erra cinema, the symbol of Communism – the sickle and the hammer – are celebrated; and if the genre would have had its way, it would have added a gun to the mix. The protagonist turns to violence upon learning a new ideology and channels their anger to eliminate the upper-caste villain. The protagonist doesn't become a masked vigilante, like they do in Hollywood.

Their identity is still the same, the violence has their name on it, but now, the protagonist doles out justice by setting up parallel courts, celebrates the red flag of the Communist parties, and denounces the state.

There is another clear marker of Erra cinema – the antithesis to the protagonist. Not the villain, but an honest officer who has faith in the system and its workings, who believes that despite its faults, the system can work and should work. Usually, it's an upper-caste urban idealist – a definite outsider to the conflict, represented by a lawyer or police officer who understands the message of the protagonist, but hates their means. This person does not want to extract revenge on the protagonist like the evil upper-caste villains, but to punish the protagonist using the constitution and the government: the institutions that the protagonist has rejected for the sake of Marxist and Maoist ideology.

Thus, the conflict in Erra cinema has three forces: the government, Marx, and upper-caste Hinduism. In the end, Marx is always right.

This genre isn't a niche; it was quite mainstream. And while the top tier of Heroes such as Chiranjeevi may not have embraced it, many did. For example, one of mainstream Telugu cinema's most popular directors Dasari Narayana Rao was a proponent of the films in this genre. Rao has worked with NTR and ANR, giving them some of their biggest blockbusters. Along with his drams he also contributed to Erra cinema. Rao made Heroes using this genre, while also contributing to it.

In his film *Orey Rikshaw* (You There, Rikshaw Driver) with R. Narayana Murthy, the protagonist, a hand-pulled rikshaw driver, fights against an MLA who betrays the protagonist and his loyal voters consisting of rikshaw pullers and their families. When all political parties have betrayed him, the red flags give the rickshaw driver a legitimate political platform. Dasari Narayana Rao also directed *Osey Ramulamma* (You There, Ramulamma) starring another Hero, Vijayashanthi, in which she plays a young Dalit woman who, after being raped by a local zamindar and almost raped by his son, resorts to armed struggle to rid herself and her village of the tormentors. Krishna, a Hero from the previous generation, added credibility to the genre by playing the role of an honest CBI officer in this film.

Mohan Babu one of the Telugu cinema's finest character actors, also did a film within the genre. It was called *Adavilo Anna* (The Naxalite in the Forest). While the word *anna* means 'brother' in Telugu, Naxalites too are called *anna*. R. Narayana Murthy added more films in this genre – *Errodu* (The Red One), *Erra Samudram* (The Sea of Red). Another Telugu actor turned politician – Roja – teamed up with Ramya Krishnan in the film *Sammakka Saarakka* in which they play sisters named after the Telangana Goddesses Sammakka and Saarakka. This film, along with its caste undertones, is a celebration of Telangana culture at a time when the movement was dormant in the popular imagination. Even *Sindhooram* (Vermillion Red), directed by Krishna Vamsi, is a stylish addition to this genre, with Jazz influences in its music and the low-budget shaky camera movements worked in the film's favour.

Since the '80s and '90, however, the genre has died a slow death. It isn't just because of the monotony created by cinema screens being flooded with the genre in a span of a two decades. The story of Erra cinema, its rise, its fall is also the story of the changing power dynamics of caste within the state. It's about the state feeling betrayed by the Naxalite. It's the story of how the film industry has become resilient to new types of cinemas, turning it into an oligopoly.

It's the story of how R. Narayana Murthy became irrelevant.

Who Killed R. Narayana Murthy?

Suspect Number 1
Reddys First: Red Next

Let's begin the investigation with *Arjun Reddy.*

Enough has been said and written about the film. The film's protagonist, Arjun, is abusive, misogynistic, and an all-round terrible human being. This much has been understood. Even his Hindi counterpart, Kabir, did not differ much. Critics have panned the character and his characterization. The director, Sandeep Reddy, has been equally criticized for coming to the defence of the two characters.

However, there are two important aspects of *Arjun Reddy* that have not been adequately discussed. First, about the film's star, Vijay Devarakonda. His quick rise to stardom has made him the face of a new generation of the Telugu film watchers – urban; tired of a generation of stars representing nepotism; disillusioned by their educational choices and careers; and somehow retaining a deep sense of hyper masculinity. Devarakonda is a good-looking guy; the camera loves him. Unlike many Telugu stars, he's not shy and does not fake humility. Other Telugu stars usually stay away from public eye to maintain a clean image – like princes afraid to mingle with commoners – and seem reluctant to be seen even during promotional events. But Vijay Devarakonda speaks his mind, uses cuss words, dances on the stage like he couldn't care less what people think about him. He can also take a joke: when he was trolled for his singing, he shared the memes that mocked him. All this already makes Vijay Devarakonda hard not to love. But there's one more aspect that has made him so damn lovable: he brandishes his Telangana accent like a sword.

Other stars have used the Telangana accent too – but as more of a gimmick. When NTR Jr and Mahesh Babu spoke in the accent, it was clearly playing to the gallery, as if doing the audience a favour. It sounded artificial, like a plate of Hyderabad biriyani served in a seven-star hotel. When not used as a gimmick by stars catering to their fans from Telangana, a caricatured version of the accent would be served to villains before they were beaten. This 'clipped' Telugu accent is usually a stand in for the accent spoken in the more developed coastal regions of Andhra Pradesh.

There are cultural factors that contribute to this widespread reluctance to use Telangana slang, dialect and accents – largely to do with the notion of purity attributed to the Telugu spoken in coastal Andhra, while those spoken in Telangana and the southern region of Rayalaseema are seen as 'impure' and 'crude'. The idea of purity also gets 'validation' from the argument that the version of the Telugu spoken in Telangana and Rayalaseema borrow words liberally from Urdu and Tamil/Kannada, respectively, owing to historical and geographical reasons. While this observation is true, the idea that Telugu, lacking such influences, is more pure falls flat in light of the fact that it is a language that has evolved due to its liberal tendency to borrow words from other languages.

Telangana accent, dialect and slang have always been as pure as any other form of the Telugu. And now, in the mouth of Vijay Devarakonda, it has become cool to speak in the accent – no longer a gimmick. There's a scene in *Arjun Reddy* which is absent in *Kabir Singh*. According to the director, the scene was edited out because of length requirements. It might have also been that *Kabir Singh* lacked the original subtext, because Shahid Kapoor just doesn't represent the same thing that Vijay Devarakonda does.

Arjun and his friend, Shiva, are meeting a potential groom for Shiva's sister. Shiva is quite fond of his would-be brother-in-law. When they finally meet Arjun and the groom opens his mouth, it turns out that he's an absolute ... misogynist. In the eyes of Arjun Reddy, while his own actions are pardonable, the groom's are not. Unlike the groom, Reddy doesn't objectify women or pass cheap comments. But the groom talks about unwaxed arms, air hostesses being old and other crude things. Then, Arjun does the most Arjun

Reddy-esque thing. In front of Shiva's potential brother-in-law, he convinces Shiva out of the alliance. The groom is horrified at Reddy's ability to scrape away at his legitimacy and dominance as a brother-in-law. As Arjun insists, Shiva begins to rethink. And then comes the moment.

The Telangana moment.

The groom, when he realizes that Shiva has been convinced to call off the wedding, says 'My mother kept telling me to be wary about these Telangana types—' Both Arjun and Shiva give him a death glare before he can complete the sentence. Arjun and Shiva are equally angry. They are both equally offended by the comment. But the camera focusses on Arjuns' face. Bang in the centre of the screen – the Hero from Telangana.

Vijay Devarakonda, the hero who speaks in the 'impure' Telugu of the region, ensures that nobody speaks ill about the new state that has so often been side-lined within cinema. The new state has found a new Hero, who will speak in its language and will not be reduced to a joke. He will get angry, he will romance pretty women, but most importantly, he will be proud of the fact that he comes from Telangana. This young hero may not be interested in politics, but his existence is political. It is not a coincidence that the coolest young Telugu hero came from Telangana two years after it was formed in 2014.

A Hero can do things like that – make the 'uncool' cool, being at the centre of screen. He didn't just turn up and represent Telangana like capsicum forced into a salad. He made it the centre of attention by merely being in the centre.

The second aspect of *Arjun Reddy* that has gone largely unnoticed is the nature of Arjun's *anger*. It feels inorganic and unearned. The guy is an academic genius, a great medical professional, his family is abundant in wealth, he has great friends, he's also a great goalkeeper. Yet, the man is angry – unnaturally so. He doesn't turn to anger after the love of his life is snatched away from him. *He has always been angry.*

This is not to say that the wealthy and the privileged can't be afflicted by poor mental health, but Arjun Reddy's constant simmering anger does not seem to justified within the plot of the film.

Except, of course, to *Telugu viewers*.

The explanation is not in any scene or any dialogue. Those are distractions. Like the reveal in great whodunnit, the source of Arjun's anger stares the audience in the face from the get-go. It just takes a while for it to dawn.

It's in the title.

Arjun *Reddy*.

The Reddy caste.

The Reddy surname has a subgenre within the Telugu cinema: Arjun Reddy got *Arjun Reddy*, Samarasimha Reddy got *Samarasimha Reddy*, Aadikeshava Reddy got *Aadi*, Bharathasimha Reddy got *Bharathasimha Reddy*, Indrasena Reddy got *Indra*. It's not just men; Reddy women get films named after themselves too: in *Shailaja Reddy Alludu* (Shailaja Reddy's Son-in-Law), *Kadapa Reddama* (Reddama from Kadapa).

These 'Reddy' films have several common features. The characters are always masculine, almost hypermasculine – regardless of whether they are a man or a woman. They are the embodiment of anger and resort to violence to assert this masculinity. Even the violence is not ordinary violence: it's hyper-violence.

Take *Arjun Reddy*. During his college days, a rivalry on the football field becomes an excuse to become angry, violent and deranged. He doesn't just want to win the match; he wants to kill the opponent. A football match, a classroom, friends, love, Preethi, his body (which he destroys in the name of love) … they all become a canvas upon which he paints his masculinity with rage.

Take the film *Aadi*, starring NTR Jr. The protagonist, Aadikeshava Reddy, or Aadi, is on the run with his uncle after his parented are murdered. Aadi's parents wanted to distribute their property amongst the poor and the downtrodden, but the evil zamindar from the neighbouring village kills them before that can happen. Aadi and his uncle run away from the village, because the zamindar doesn't want the male heir to survive. It's tense; the two are clearly outnumbered and it's night-time. Aadi is a stranger to these parts, and his uncle is old. The goons have been ruthless with his parents, and Aadi and his uncle seem to stand no chance. At one point, as the uncle insists on continuing to flee, Aadi stops in his tracks – tired of running. He turns around and faces the goons for the first time. Sick of his uncle's cowardice, Aadi takes out a local handmade bomb and hurls them towards the goons. In the lush green fields, some of the goons explode into tiny blobs of flesh. Now Aadi takes a step towards the one left standing. 'Come and get me if you can.' The goons are terrified; they haven't seen anything like this. They run back and for the first time, Aadi is the one chasing the villains with a handmade bomb in his hand. Eventually, all the villains meet the same violent end. Aadi has now become a man by slaying his enemies.

For those unfamiliar with the film, Aadi is only *eight* years old when all of this unfolds. The hypermasculinity and the penchant for violence does not even spare the Reddy children.

Another feature of 'Reddy' cinema is that the protagonist is almost always a saviour. When the film is set in a village, the protagonist owns large tracts of land and lives like a quasi-king and looks after his people; when it is named after a revolutionary – like in *George Reddy* – the setting is a university campus. In *Arjun Reddy*, he is a genius doctor – a literal saviour. While all Indian male protagonists are saviours, what differentiates the 'Reddy' cinema is that the caste is pronounced. The film titles have the surname; when the protagonist speaks his name there is an emphasis on the 'Reddy'; and most importantly; the Reddy is never an equal to anybody. They are *above* and are beneficiaries of relationships where they are superior to those around them.

So *Arjun Reddy* is an asshole to his friends because he is *better*. In *Indra*, Chiranjeevi sacrifices his lands for the sake of a dam for the drought-ridden people; in *Sye Raa Narasimha Reddy*, he saves people from the British occupation. So audacious is the claim in the latter

film, that it argues that before the First War of Independence that
began with the likes of Jhansi Laxmi Bai in 1857, it *really* began when
a Reddy fought against the British.

But why are the Reddys – more precisely, the Reddy films –
suspects in the metaphorical death of R. Narayana Murthy and Erra
cinema?

Those who carry the Reddy surname are members of the Reddy
caste, a powerful people within the Telugu society. While primarily
a farming class, their position in the Hindu *varna* system is murky.
There have been Reddy kings, commanders, businessmen; Reddys
have been zamindars and farmers; and the Reddy surname also finds
itself as a suffix amongst some tribes in Andhra Pradesh, even though
Chief Minister Jagan Mohan Reddy is a Christian.

While their historical genealogy is murky, it is their role within
post-Independence Andhra that defines their importance to the
region and its cinema. Here's a list of all the chief ministers of the
state since its formation in 1956.

1. Neelam Sanjeeva *Reddy* - Congresss
2. Damodaram Sanjeevayya - Congress
3. Kasu Brahmananda *Reddy* - Congress
4. P.V. Narasaimha Rao - Congress
5. Jalagam Vengala Rao - Congress
6. Marri Chenna *Reddy* - Congress
7. Tanguturi Anjaiah - Congress
8. Bhavanam Venkatarami *Reddy* - Congress
9. Kotla Vijayabhaskara *Reddy* - Congress
10. N.T. Rama Rao – Telugu Desam Party
11. Nadendla Bhaskara Rao - Telugu Desam Party
12. N. Janaradhana Reddy - Congress
13. N. Chandhrababu Naidu - Telugu Desam Party
14. Y.S. Rajashekhara *Reddy* - Congress
15. K. Rossiah - Congress

16. N. Kiran Kumar *Reddy* - Congress
17. Jagan Mohan *Reddy* (Post 2014 Andhra Pradesh) - Y.S.R. Congress Party

When you read the list, two obvious factors stick out: the huge number of Reddy chief ministers, and that they all belong to the Indian National Congress. The Reddys have held dominant political positions within the state and have managed to reorganize political capital and social location through these positions. In 1956, after the first general election in the newly formed state, they controlled 35 per cent of the minister portfolios. They dominate in the Telangana and the Rayalaseema region in the south. Even the early panchayat elections held at the village level were dominated by Reddys; this, in turn, laid the foundation for the dominance of the Reddy caste in state politics over the next few decades. The disproportionate representation is worse than it already seems in light of the damning statistic that the Reddys made up only about 6.5 per cent of the then unified state.

The early pioneers in Telugu cinema belonged to the Reddy caste and were beneficiaries of the caste's dominance in the political sphere. They were university-educated Reddys who made black-and-white social dramas, folklore films, mythological fantasies. But the Reddy surname can be confusing, because all Reddys are not 'Reddy', i.e., there are those with the surname don't necessarily belong to the caste. The Reddys that are spoken about in the 'Reddy' films are the socially powerful Reddys, with high political capital.

The most popular Reddy of this millennium, Y.S. Rajashekhara Reddy (Y.S.R.), was known for his supposed magnanimity in dealing with the outlawed Maoists. In 2005, he invited Maoists for talks to 'settle the issue' once and for all. He too belonged to the Congress Party.

'After so many years of fighting, what the bloody hell do you guys even want' he seemed to ask.

In a highly publicized affair, top Maoist leaders were invited to hold talks with the government. They were put up in the plush Manjeera Guest House owned by the government. The Telugu daily *Eenadu* mocked the Maoists who were invited talks by showing waiters in posh restaurants who were confused by the culinary demands of their outlawed guests. The talks were a spectacular failure and in one of the meetings of the Central Regional Bureau (CBR) of the Communist Party of India (Maoist) noted:

'...Congress made a lot of promises that the Naxalite problem is a socio-economic problem, that it is not possible to solve it through encounters that it is against fake encounters and that it would conduct judicial enquiry on the fake encounters that took place in Chandrababu's rule. **But it broke all the promises.** It started obstructing the meetings of the revolutionaries since November. It started encounters from January. **After a gap of eight months the Y.S.R government started direct war... Like during the rule of Chandrababu Naidu, the state of A.P. has turned to be a police state.**' [text in bold done by the author]

In Erra cinema there was a clear threat because the figures that were the 'villains' were the powerful zamindar Reddys. But the more irksome aspect of Erra cinema was that the 'Hero' who saved the people wasn't a Reddy. It was for the first time someone from the tribes. Or a Dalit man. Or a Dalit woman. The protagonist became a savior when they became Naxalite. That in itself was revolutionary.

In 2009, Y.S.R. was re-elected a second time. But on September 2nd, the helicopter that he took off in Hyderabad, crashed in the Nallamalla forests of Andhra – the very place that was the hiding place for Maoists and 'suspected' Maoists. The might of the Indian state was deployed to search for the crash site of the helicopter – police personnel, Greyhound cops who specialized in forest terrain and were known to wipe out the Naxal 'infestation' in Andhra Pradesh, more choppers – everything was put to use.

And ultimately, the government took help of local tribe members to find the body of the former chief minister and his plane.

Eventually, Congress lost elections in the state over the Telangana issue. Y.S.R.'s son Jagan Mohan Reddy formed the Y.S.R. Congress after splitting with the Congress. Along with Jagan Mohan Reddy, the Reddys deserted the Congress in favour of Y.S.R. Congress. The Congress which won 33 seats out of the possible forty-two in United Andhra Pradesh in 2009 was wiped out of both Telangana and new Andhra Pradesh.

The Reds may not have taken care of the Reddys, but the revenge came from the forest.

But the Reddy caste also had other enemies who were jealous of their success. Reddys were the ones with political power and another community had found a Hero who was willing to do their work. The Reddys had used their political might in cinema, but for the first-time cinema and a Hero were going to be used to gain political might.

Suspect Number 2
Betrayal of the Kammas

Like Rome, all roads in Telugu cinema and politics inevitably lead to NTR, even the highway of caste. NTR was a fantastic actor. NTR played Lord/divine Krishna so well, Krishna probably looks like him, that's how good an actor he was. NTR was the Chief Minister who stood for Telugu pride. NTR was the leader of Opposition in the Parliament in 1984 because when Indira Gandhi was assassinated, Telugu voters refused to sway to emotion and stuck to the man they trusted. The Telugu Hero, NTR.

But NTR was also 'Kamma'. He belonged to the Kamma caste.

The Kammas are a prosperous caste found mostly in Andhra, but they are splintered across Tamil Nadu, Karnataka and in the last five decades or so even the United States of America. Their caste rivalry with the Reddys spills over into the foreign lands where the Telugu Association for North America (TANA) is accused of playing favouritism with Kammas and in response the Reddys in 1991 started the American Telugu Association (ATA). A more embarrassing and direct testament to their conflict was brought to light by Markandey Katju where he observed a cricket match played in the USA between Reddy XI and Kamma XI.

The match was abandoned because of quarrel that broke out between the two teams.

While in the traditional Hindu varna caste-ranking system, Kammas are shudras, their social positioning has changed because of their role in history where they played the parts of army commanders, chieftains of large areas, and local kings. They were soldiers under Kakatiya Kings who ruled parts of the Telugu states between 10th and twelfth century. When the kings of the Vijayangara Empire in the seventeenth and eighteenth century wanted to attack Tamil kings they used Kamma soldiers which explains their presence in the southernmost state. Their prosperity can be traced to the fertile Godavari delta in Andhra Pradesh where they reaped the riches of being a farming community. Unlike, the powerful Reddys who generally owned land in arid regions, Kammas gravitated towards the Godavari Delta. Even the kings found it beneficial to marry into the Kamma farming community owing to their domination over agricultural resources. A highly adaptable community prospered more than other 'conquered' members under the later Muslims rulers as they were granted the title of 'Chowdhary' – under which they would collect taxes on behalf of the Muslim rulers. Even under the British they benefitted from the multiple irrigation projects that were set up by the colonial masters, as the Kamma caste members continued to hold control of agricultural land. They were expert rice cultivators who continued to increase the quantity of land they possessed by taking part in 'agricultural colonization'.

The rich landlord would first either by force or dubious economic practices take away lands from small peasants or tribesmen who lived on fertile land. They would either pay low rates of compensation to the peasants or snatch it away by asking for documentation as recognized by a government that was in collusion with the Kammas. Driven out of their own land and with no other forms of employment, the new landless peasants and tribes would be forced to work under Kamma landlords and toil away for generations.

This practice would become the plot for many of R. Narayana Murthy's films and Erra cinema.

According to researcher Dalel Benbabaali, the caste owns over 85 per cent of agricultural land in the fertile Godavari Delta. They form roughly 5 per cent of the population of the Telugu states.

The surpluses from agriculture led to investments in other industries and even today many Telugu industrialists and prosperous NRIs belong to the Kamma caste. The community also invested in cinema which would explain why three of the biggest families in Telugu cinema belong to the caste – NTR, ANR and Daggubati Ramanaidu, the owner of the most successful production company in the film industry.

But the more damning characteristic of the caste's legacy is that three generations later, it is still the very same families that run and profit from the industry. Even a later entrant to the pantheon of Telugu cinema Heroes – Krishna and his son Mahesh Babu – belong to the Kamma caste.

Although the Kamma caste has always been socially powerful, they had to wait and snatch the political power from the Reddys at the opportune moment. For decades after independence the Reddys ruled over the state using the Congress party as their primary weapon.

The wealthy Kammas had to wait for their own Hero, NTR.

It helped that NTR was seen as a pan-caste figure who represented the inclusive term 'Telugu' to connect with all sections of society.

While NTR didn't directly challenge the Brahmin hierarchy like his counterparts in Tamil Nadu, films in the second half of his career glorify a protagonist who challenges upper-caste hegemony.

Daana Veera Soora Karna (The Benevolent and Brave Hero Karna), released in the January of 1977, is a film that narrates the event of the *Mahabharatha* from the perspective of Karna, the prince who was abandoned by his royal mother and was forced to live the life of a chariot driver's son. Even when playing the role of a 'lower' caste character NTR chose the one character who *really* was upper caste i.e., the tragedy of Karna was that he was a prince who was forced to face the harsh life of a 'lower' caste chariot driver as opposed to the tragedy being the oppressiveness of the caste system. Even the character who denounces the caste system in favour of Karna is the upper caste Duryodhana who despite his genuine affection for Karna has ulterior motives.

But the film itself is a testament to the audacity and the bulldozing power NTR had over Telugu cinema. NTR plays three different roles in the film – Lord Krishna, Duryodhana and Karna with more importance given to the friendship between the latter two – a first of its kind. The film was shot in record forty-three days to release ahead of another film titled *Kurukshetram* which had similar themes. The film's most popular dialogue, which was written in chaste Telugu, directly questioned the sanctity and caste-based rigidity that the Pandavas and Kauravas, the warring upper-caste cousins of Mahabharatha, adhere to. The Pandavas are deliberately shown in bad light.

This was also a direct challenge to two caste groups that were dominating politics within the state – the Reddys and Brahmins – both the castes that controlled state politics. Andhra Pradesh had its first Brahmin Chief Minister in P.V. Narasimha Rao whose tenure only lasted for two years and was seen as a puppet chief minister in the hands of Congress party who ran operations from Delhi. The '70s would see four chief Ministers and one year of President's rule in the state.

The year 1977 saw another challenge to the government from NTR. This time the challenge was thrown not just to the state government, but he was punching upwards, specifically towards North – where the gods reside in the skies and – where the God of the Congress party, Indira Gandhi ran operations from.

The film titled *Yamagola* (Hellish Chaos) came out in the October of the year.

The real protagonist of the film is not NTR's character Satyam – but Lord Yama himself, the Hindu god of Death and the king of hell.

The set-up of the film is simple. A young honest man, Satyam, whose name literally means Truth faces against a village Panchayat president, Rudrayya. The two are at loggerheads. Satyam belongs to the honest, working class (caste is suspiciously hidden), while Rudrayya is rich, corrupt and is an oppressor in the village.

So far, familiar.

Satyam and Rudrayya's daughter are madly in love and Rudrayya opposes the alliance. So far extremely familiar.

But the real twist arises when Rudrayya plots to kill Satyam. And he's successful.

The hero dies barely one hour into the film and is first taken to heaven by divine escorts. Unlike an 'expected' reaction after one's own death, Satyam is amused. He greets the escorts saying 'glad to meet you' and calls them 'brother'. Once in heaven he even dances with the divine escorts. And the real arguments of the film begin when Satyam confronts a few dead Brahmin priests who are adamant about preserving caste hierarchies even in heaven.

NTR mocks them for their rigidity.

Then he meets Indra – the king of gods – himself. And it's an iconic moment – the champion of the Telugu people facing gods.

NTR had made a career out of thrashing villains from all walks of life and now the villains on earth had become too small for him.

Only gods were left for him to vanquish because when NTR walks into heaven he finds out that it is in disarray and is run by an incompetent despot who reached the highest office through nepotism. This was in 1977. Two years after Indira Gandhi had declared the Emergency. Satyam is then immediately banished by Indra from heaven to hell for speaking the truth.

And it is in hell, that the real fun begins. The *gola* (chaos) unravels.

Hell, like heaven, is in a bad place. It's hell for not just sinners who've made their way there, but also those working there. Satyam soon realizes that the imps who work in hell have been working there for *yugas* (eons) without any break, they are overworked and underpaid, they haven't unionized, and more importantly, there are no female imps to handle female sinners. Satyam soon infuses Leftist ideology into the imps and becomes the leader of the first Trade union in hell. He even argues that once female imps are employed, they should get maternity leave too.

Satyam refers to other imps as 'Comrade'. And he even uses the slogan coined and used by Telugu revolutionaries: *Viplavam Varthilalli* (Long Live the Revolution).

It's image creation of literal mythic proportions. NTR liberating dark-skinned short men, who speak simple Telugu, by introducing them to Leftist thought as they chant his name.

It's also commentary on what heaven and hell *really* look like. Heaven is being run in the North (representing the central government in Delhi and Heaven) by corrupt beneficiaries of nepotism who are upper caste and regressive. They even speak a 'different' language that demarcates their class. Arcane language, full of Sanskrit whereas Satyam uses English words liberally, treats others equally by calling them 'brother' (something NTR did even in real life), and uses simple Telugu spoken by the masses.

Hell was full of overworked men and oppressed women, who needed someone to teach them how to organize and speak for them i.e., in need of a saviour, someone who came from a different world.

When Satyam confronts Yama, the God of Death is shown as a hardworking, law-abiding God unlike other gods who mortals depend on, such as Varuna (God of Rain, who is criticized for being shoddy at his job), Agni and Vayu (gods of Fire and Wind, who collude and set fire to houses of the poor and destroy them), and Kubera (God of Wealth, who has been hoarding abundant divine black money). The metaphor Satyam uses to compare the gods is that of 'Ministries' – each gods represents a ministry that they work for and only Yama is seen as hardworking, but aged and overworked with increasing number of sinners. Yama is a metaphor for the overworked judiciary in the country – trying hard, but left to fend for itself after corrupt MPs, MLAs and bureaucrats have destroyed the country.

At some point NTR directly takes a dig at Sanjay Gandhi. A government doctor who has performed forced vasectomies is about to be meted out with the most severe punishment by Yama. Satyam argues that he could defend the unpardonable actions of the doctor. The doctor reveals that he was forced to perform these vasectomies as it was a mandate from the government. Yama then asks if the person behind these orders has come to hell yet, and he is told that the 'sinner's' (referring to Sanjay Gandhi) time will soon come.

Three years later, Sanjay Gandhi would die in a plane crash.

Satyam defending the government doctor has one more purpose. It's NTR asking the population that the mid- to low-level government employees were helpless and their hands were tied during the Emergency and could be forgiven. The reality of that maybe debatable, but it's NTR also securing the support of government employees within the state, while managing to critique the government.

The film then takes a comical route with *narakalokam* (hell) shutting down because of unionization and Yama coming to earth to understand the real position of people in modern India. Even the most honest God has been living in a bubble and needs a reality check and was given as much by the biggest Hero of Telugu silver screen – NTR.

Yamagola was such a big hit that it spurned its own genre of Yama films i.e. films in which an ordinary man would take on the God of Death himself. Part existential in its theme of man vs death and part satirical, this genre has found takers in Chiranjeevi in the film *Yamudiki Mogudu*[2] (The Tormentor of Yama) with a similar plotline to *Yamagola*. Chiranjeevi's film was a smash hit. NTR Jr, grandson of NTR, also resorted to this genre in *Yamadonga* (The Hellish Thief) when he needed to resurrect his career from a string of flops. Even the Telugu comedian Ali, who briefly tried his hand at being the lead in films attained stardom through the film *Yamaleela* (Yama's Play).

The biggest consequence of *Yamagola* and *Daana Veera Soora Karna* was that NTR had managed to convince the people of Andhra Pradesh that he was ready to question the government, although for now in films only. There were rumours floating that NTR would soon join politics – meanwhile in Tamil Nadu another superstar, M.G. Ramachandran, had already joined politics and had given confidence to NTR that he would be received well by Telugu voters.

But the question was, would NTR join the Congress? Would the man who once played God become a puppet?

He wouldn't.

He decided to start his own party – it was also aptly titled Telugu Desam Party. Its agenda was clear. Unlike the Congress, this one worked for the interests of the Telugu people. But, while NTR was a pan-Andhra figure, he still needed a community to help him battle the political and electoral might of the Congress. His charisma would attract large crowds, he did have the popular support of the Backward

---

2   While the word *'mogudu'* means husband in colloquial Telugu, in this context it means 'tormentor'.

Caste (BC) in the state and his goodwill might have even made him a guaranteed candidate in whichever constituency he contested in, but to be an alternative to the Congress required financial and political capital.

That's when the caste he belonged to helped him.

While the Reddys had firm grip on the Congress, the wealthy Kammas had found for the first time a way to organize themselves into political capital. They could re-engineer Telugu society if they came into power. NTR had a powerful team of Kamma men who worked to boost his image. First there was the power of Ramoji Rao, the Telugu media baron akin to Rupert Murdoch, who owns the Telugu daily *Eenadu*. While it was one of the most popular dailies, *Eenadu* tirelessly churned news articles to promote NTR, then an experienced Kamma leader in the Congress, and Chandrababu Naidu a young leader in the Congress switched sides to join the Telugu Desam Party. Two years before setting up the party, Chandrababu Naidu, had married NTR's daughter and that resulted in an alliance between two powerful Kammas. All of this political machinery resulted in NTR swearing in as Andhra Pradesh's first non-Congress chief minister. There was faith in NTR's populist promises. Rice for two rupees a kilo. Inheritance rights for women. Telugu-Ganga water project for the arid southern region of Rayalaseema.

But there was also a sense of betrayal about his regime as a chief minister. For all of NTR's campaign on Telugu pride and importance of a unified Telugu society, there was clear caste favouritism. NTR was a Telugu man who spoke about Telugu pride. But he was also a Kamma man under whom the Kammas became even more powerful. And this did not go unnoticed by the Telugu society.

There was the murder of popular Kapu leader Vangaveeti Mohan Ranga Rao who was from the Congress. His close coterie prospered economically. But one incident clearly highlights NTR's bias.

It's not even an incident it was a massacre. It took place in the village of Kaaramchedu on July 16, 1985. The village is famous for its prosperous Kammas and multiple film personalities hail from the village. It is this same village that Rana Daggubati's family hails from.

These are broadly the events that transpired. Two Kamma youth tried to wash their buffalos in the fresh water source of Madigapalle, a village with predominantly Madiga population, a Dalit caste. When a Madiga boy, Katti Chandriah stood up to them, the Kamma youth almost assaulted the boy. Then another Madiga woman Munnagi Suvaartha, stood up for the boy and threatened the Kamma youth by hitting them with the vessel in her hand.

Enraged by the courage shown by a Dalit woman, the Kamma men of Kaaramchedu village, upon hearing that their youth were attacked resorted to unparalleled violence the next day. They raided Madigapalle and destroyed the huts, axed the men, and physically and sexually assaulted the women of the village.

Officially six Madiga men were killed. They were Duddu Moshe, Duddu Ramesh, Tella Yehoshua, Tella Moshe, Tella Muthaiah and Duddu Abraham. Unofficially there might have been more, and police played their hand in covering up the crimes of Kamma men. The mastermind behind the crime was Daggubati Chenchu Ramiah whose son was NTR's son-in- law.

It wasn't that caste-based atrocities by upper caste men were new to the state, but it was that NTR had stood for something different, and he turned out to be no different from the Reddys of earlier decades.

The man who dared to criticize Indira Gandhi, the man whose promise was Telugu pride, the man who apparently reformed heaven, hell and everything in between couldn't punish the crimes of men from his own caste and family. Life had come a full circle for NTR From raising questions in *Yamagola* he would become the very authority he criticized – out of touch with reality and displaying clear favouritism.

NTR's tenure would later become infamous for quasi-judicial killings of 'Naxalites'. Police officers were given a free hand to round up 'suspected' Naxalites, farcical conspiracy cases were slapped on individuals and Adivasi tribes bore the brunt of the activities to crush the rising Naxalite movement.

NTR would soon lose the elections on 1989. When re-elected later in 1994, he would rule for less than a year, before getting ousted from his own party by Chandrababu Naidu.

Daggubati Chenchu Ramiah, the man said to be behind the Karamchedu massacre was eventually killed by Naxalites. The very group that a hero like R. Narayana Murthy and Erra cinema glorified. The powerful Kammas, who had found political power in the state through NTR, the affluent Kammas, who owned film production houses, were actors and owned media outlets, the Kammas who defined the fabric of Telugu culture by the '80s, witnessed a counter-narrative develop in the popular imagination through Erra cinema whose rise began in that decade, and represented the dominant castes in a poor light. And a Hero like R. Narayana Murthy made the villains in the Kamma story – the Naxalites, Adivasis and Dalits – the Heroes.

It might not have been a revolution, but it was revolutionary.

Suspect Number 3
The Left Parties: An Inside Job

When I was twelve years old, I was at the forefront of a revolt. A revolt that was merely confined to a classroom. But in my twelve-year-old mind I was a Bolshevist rubbing shoulders with Lenin, I was in Tianmen Square facing military tanks as they rolled on, I was storming the Bastille waiting to guillotine the monarchs.

Except, in my case it was against the teachers in my class.

The bone of contention was a free period that had freed up in the timetable because a teacher had taken a vacation for a month. A substitute teacher, who was supposed to take the class, and was probably overworked, wasn't too keen on conducting the class during the week. She wanted to use the free class to correct pending assignments from her other classes. And her solution was simple: send the girls of the class to the library while the boys were forced to stay indoors and be silent and finish untouched homework in other subjects. It was a haphazard solution by a tired teacher who prioritized stabbing her red pen on the answer sheets in front of her.

At first, like dogs that sensed a thief, the boys barked about the injustice, but it soon was reduced to a whimper. The second day, rumours began to spread that the girls weren't 'actually' in the library and were playing games. And even those in the library weren't finishing homework, but whiling their time away reading the *Harry Potter* books.

This time the protests from the boys rose in their anger levels and sincerity. But a threat to call the principal into the class, ensured that our rising sense of rebellion drained away. The teacher took glee and her strokes with the red pen got more violent.

The third day, the girls mocked the boys. And, worse, the teacher joined in. Young masculinity was bruised. Before we could get angry, again the threat of the principal was evoked. It was utter humiliation; our faces were flush with blood and cheeks redder than the papers underneath my teacher's pen. How could I, the young boy who felt the revolutionary spirit of all the Telugu Heroes, succumb to the injustice in front of me?

And on the fourth day, I saw *Rang De Basanti* (Paint Me the Colour of Spring), the Hindi film with an ensemble cast of Aamir Khan, Soha Ali Khan, Siddharth, Madhavan, Atul Kulkarni, and Kunal Kapoor. In it, a band of young aimless college-going men, who are dispassionate and disillusioned by the country are brought together by a foreign documentary filmmaker who is keen on recreating the greatness of the revolutionary freedom fighters.

No peaceful Gandhis or the Moderate Gokhales for her. Bhagat Singh. Azad. Ram Prasad Bismil. She went for the martyrs and for the spirit they embodied. Young and willing to die. And angry.

In these aimless men, she sees potential actors for her part-fiction part-footage documentary. When one of their sincere pilot friends sacrifices his life and is still labelled incompetent by crooked ministers, the men are forced to look inward and become as revolutionary as the characters they portray. A brilliant *masala* trope that galvanized the youth of the nation to look inward – into history – to bring about external change.

More importantly, it legitimized the bubbling rage of a twelve-year-old who too was witnessing injustice unfold in front of his eyes. Except, who could I look up to? My situation was different. I was young. Telugu boy. I needed my own heroes. The angry ones. While the ones on screen did fight against injustice, their fictitiousness was palpable. They came with their own background music. I had no way to match that.

I needed to find a real Hero. Someone who was at least a little bit like me.

In a corner bookshelf of the library, the very place the 'enemy' frolicked, while the boys toiled away in classrooms, I found a small book that spoke about Tarimala Nagireddy aka Comrade TN. He was a Telugu man. He too, like me, was from Anantapur District in Andhra Pradesh. But more importantly, he was a Communist leader, so committed to the cause of economic and social equality, that he eventually rebelled against his own father and redistributed hundreds of acres of land to the poor. He took part in the Telangana armed struggle and was arrested. According to a popular anecdote, after his death in 1976 at the age of fifty, when thousands thronged to see their frail fallen Comrade, the government forced doctors to perform autopsy on the body to confirm whether he was really dead or not.

Comrade TN put fear in authority even after his death, while amassing love from the people.

Comrade TN felt like the Hero I was looking for. I took the letters of my own names and labelled myself Comrade MM. This was my

Rang De Basanti moment – except my colour of choice was red rather than the colour of spring.

I mustered the inspiration of Comrade TN and walked into the class the next day. When the injustice continued, I walked up to the door to walk out. At first the teacher was puzzled. She wasn't expecting any student to see such an injustice in her actions, let alone start a mini mutiny. But I did. She tried holding me back. The other boys in the class supported my actions through hoots or laughter. Noticing this, she yelled at all of us and asked us to sit down. When I resisted, she tried to force me to sit down in the front bench opposite hers by holding me by my shoulders and pushing me down onto my seat. The class gasped. Comrade MM's revolutionary spirit, egged on by the imaginary ghost of Comrade TN, tried to wrestle out of the grip of the teacher. The teacher continued to try and muscle me back into my seat. As I struggled, my leg unwittingly kicked the bench in front of me causing the teacher's bench to topple. Papers flew, her files were flung as far as the doorway, and her bag collapsed on the floor causing white chalk-dust to rise like smoke at a funeral.

The sound of two tables crashing and falling echoed across the whole room and stunned the class into silence. I was horror-struck, like having found out a toy gun was real. The teacher dragged me to the principal's room. I was rightfully punished by being grounded and suspended for a brief while.

Comrade MM's revolution ended with as much farce as a comedian stepping on a banana peel in a film from the '90s.

As I grew older, the memory of Comrade TN hung around me like a stain – a page in a book buried in a library. But I could never put a face to him. Neither were his faces plastered across Anantapur, nor did Telugu society seem to remember him.

There are many reasons to this, the least of which is that as a young boy I may have imposed greatness onto Comrade TN.

But even the parties on the left seemed to have ignored him. The disappearance of the face of Comrade TN from the politics of the

Left in the Telugu states connects itself to the same question that all political parties in the region grapple with: whose is the correct face?

Every political party has Heroes they worship. They are usually printed on top of every hoarding at party meetings, solitary heads that hang suspended in ink. They range from thinkers, freedom fighters and politicians as parties aim to convince voters that the best of the past shall be distilled for the politics of the future. Underneath their photos are the images of new *netas* and the giant party name all splashed in garish colours that represent the party. The Reds and Whites for the Congress. The Yellows for the TDP. The Blues and Greens for the YSR Congress and the Orange for Pawan Kalyan.

When the Congress Party gathers, one usually sees the head of Mahatma Gandhi, Nehru, Indira Gandhi and Rajiv Gandhi. NTR, a leader who rose on populist thought and cinematic dialogues and speeches, didn't have the history, the intellectual backing or the intellectuals that the Congress appropriated; therefore, he plastered his own face on almost all hoardings. It was his face that became the image of the campaign – decades of cultivated fame and image management had made him the be all and end all – common man, revolutionary and God.

Decades later, Chiranjeevi had a similar issue, when he started his own political party, Praja Rajyam Party. Voters had wizened up to not trust one face only. He plastered the faces of Gandhi and Ambedkar and then sensing that they were too broad figures he added Phule, the anti-caste reformer. As a way to represent his own philanthropy, Chiranjeevi added Mother Teresa too on the poster.

The parties on the Left in Andhra, Communist Party of India (CPI) and Communist Party of India (Marxist) and the once banned Communist Party of India (Maoist) were once very powerful. Although never in complete control of the state government, their rallies as late as 2004 attracted over a million people. But the faces the parties depended on still remained the same: Mao, Marx, and occasionally Lenin.

In a post-liberalization Andhra Pradesh, the Telugu states required new faces, homegrown faces to connect to a new generation that had become a little more urban, a little more aspirational in their dreams, and a little greedier for material wealth. The urban rich found Chandrababu Naidu as the pioneer of these new aspirations, the rural poor found a voice in Y.S.R. in 2004 after he walked as much as the length of the state, but the Left threw no new leaders or appeared to have a clue on how to tackle the urban nature of the new voters.

This reflected even in cinema. Chiranjeevi began the trend for the hero to move from the rural interiors to urban areas – the family values remained the same, the villains remained equally cruel, the levels of heroism didn't corrode. Just the hero changed his location. The heroines though began to bear the brunt of the shift. They began to be imported from the northern parts of India because urban also meant fairer, exposing more skin, looser morals.

By the nineties younger actors began to cultivate their own fans – Pawan Kalyan, Chiranjeevi's younger brother, became a famous actor himself gathering the young and rebellious crowd of the age. He came up with new hairstyles, new fashion trends, and new lingo for young people. Unlike the previous generation who romanticized an educated college going youth as a 'saviour', Pawan Kalyan's characters went to college and had fun. They failed exams, got rejected by women, hung out with friends and played cricket. They went to college because it was a thing they had to do instead of saving the 'family' or a 'village' waiting for the college-goer to weaponize his education. His early films celebrated a young urban aimlessness – resulting from a fear of expectations – youth looking Westward and armed with awkward English. This portrayal led to broad societal changes in definitions of success. Even Mahesh Babu who made his debut around the same time, with his baby face and clumpy hair, looked out of place anywhere but a city.

Compare that to Erra cinema and R. Narayana Murthy, whose films stuck to their rural roots and felt like each film belonged to an extended *erra* (Red) multiverse. R. Narayana Murthy too continued the same acting from his earlier films – his cheeks quivered like he had swallowed an earthquake that was stuck in his throat. The songs in Erra cinema sounded common and ultimately, even the message that once seemed so fresh became outdated. Audience got the message about the plight of the downtrodden, but for now they just wanted to watch a film.

It also didn't help that the Naxalite movement had taken a violent turn in response to the constant physical and ideological attacks by the government. State police and military personnel with names like 'Greyhounds' and 'Scorpions' were deployed to wipe out Naxalites. The media kept referring to the hills and mountains that were home to the Adivasis as the Red Corridor. Naxalites in response plotted an assassination attempt on the then Chief Minister of Andhra Pradesh – Chandrababu Naidu. They planted nine landmines, to kill the most powerful man in the state. The location too was iconic – near Tirupathi the abode of the supposed home deity to the Telugu people, Lord Balaji.

Chandrababu Naidu survived the assassination attempt with injuries. There is a belief that Lord Balaji is permanently paying back debt to the God of wealth, Kubera. The Chief Minister who had borrowed millions of dollars from the World Bank would find a second lease of life. Naxalites couldn't kill him if compounding interest rates couldn't.

Instead of peace being infused into the hills, violence flooded into the roads and the highways and reaching the lanes of cities. The Heroes of Erra cinema seemed to put the newfound dream towards an urban future at risk. The parties on the left had no new Heroes or faces to project, the message of Erra cinema felt outdated, R. Narayana Murthy got repetitive, the Naxalites were seen as ruthless as the police that hounded them.

This meant that Erra cinema became redundant. *People's Star* R. Narayana Murthy lost his stardom and the support of the people who had once found him fresh waned.

Being a 'Comrade' once symbolized justice, but it soon stood for violence. The works of Comrade TN, and his protégé-for-a-day Comrade MM were soon left behind by a state now hungry for new Heroes.

Suspect Number 4
The Kapus: The Almost Heroes

The Kapus suffer like middle children usually do.

They have borne the brunt of having had other farming castes – The Reddys and Kammas – succeed economically and politically. In the past, they have often found themselves voting for the Reddys and Kammas, depending on the politics of the time – always aligning, but rarely in the commanding position.

Yet, they are concerned by the political mobilization of Dalits and governments that work expressly in their favour. The '80s and '90s not only saw the dominant castes succeed, but also had Dalits finding a voice through political organizations and films. While there were films that spoke about Reddys, Kammas and Dalits, none spoke about Kapus.

The Kapus have the unique misfortune of having come second to the Hero party. They too are a predominantly farming community and historically have had political mileage. Dasari Narayana Rao, one of the biggest directors of the '80s and the '90s belonged to this caste. They also have had the backing of the biggest Hero of the modern Telugu generation in Chiranjeevi. And yet, they never managed to gain the political clout that the Kammas and Reddys did.

Chiranjeevi's political debacle is a glaring example of the way in which the Kapus have failed to capture popular imagination. If you look at Chiranjeevi's career, his political entry was almost destiny. He had taken over the cinema baton from NTR as the biggest star of the industry. (In Tamil Nadu, the same fate awaited Rajinikanth, who had taken over from M.G. Ramachandran, as the biggest cinema hero for the state. Like Chiranjeevi, Rajinikanth too teased his prospective entry into politics for almost two decades.) Chiranjeevi of the '80s was an actor before anything else. In a film such as *Vijetha* (Winner), he played the role of a seemingly aimless son, Chinnababu, who has a passion for the sport of football. Like Arjun Reddy, he is a goalkeeper. It was symbolic. Goalkeeping is a thankless position; nobody remembers the hundreds of saves the keeper makes, but one goal is let in and it is like ink spilled on a white page. Each scoresheet is a tally of how poorly the goalkeepers have fared. Chinnababu's father can only see the goals his son has let in. He has failed his exams; he has no apparent aim in life; he cares for a sport with seemingly no long-term security. Chinnababu is a great son, but his father cannot see that yet. Eventually, when the whole family abandons his father who is in desperate need of money, it is Chinnababu who saves him by becoming the man of the house. Chinnababu sells his kidney, but doesn't tell his father how he got the money. He sacrifices the sport he loves. This goalkeeper not only saves goals for his team but scores the winner and made sure another team member gets the credit. It's emotional. It's melodramatic. In the climactic portions of the film, after he's been hospitalized, the camera pans past the entire cast – reduced to tears by Chinnababu's sacrifice. It's also the film flaunting its cast. The best actors across all generations are present. They are all weeping. And yet it's only Chiranjeevi's big expressive eyes – tired, exhausted and satisfied that his father has finally accepted him – that stick with the audience.

He got a Filmfare award for it.

In the detective-comedy *Chantabbai* (Chantabbai), Chiranjeevi plays a wannabe detective Panduranga Rao aka James 'Pond' who is sent on a wild goose chase trying to prove the innocence of the woman he loves after she's been accused of murder. It begins there and ends with him trying to find the rightful heir (Chantabbai) of a businessman, when multiple men turn up claiming to be the real Chantabbai. The film is a silly goofball comedy, yet Chiranjeevi does the one thing that these comedies struggle with: he makes the audience care for 'the idiot'. James 'Pond' is silly, barely qualified and a hopeless romantic, but his sheer persistence makes him endearing. The clever dialogues and situations are the result of director–writer Jandhyala, but Chiranjeevi sells the comedic and emotional beats. Towards the end, Pandurangao Rao aka James 'Pond' realizes that he is, in fact, the real Chantabbai. In matter of one scene, Chiranjeevi has the audience weeping with him. Through the course of the film, the character has been dressed like Charlie Chaplin; stripped of all heroism, the fights reduced to comedy; humiliated in front of the woman he loves … and yet, when he recounts his experience of growing up as an orphan on the streets with an empty stomach, your blood boils not just against the father who abandoned him, but the whole world for being so cruel. When James Pond uses the Telugu insult *lanjakoduku* (bastard) to recount the abuses he heard while growing up, you want to tear the screen and give him a hug. That is the kind of calibre Chiranjeevi possesses.

But this is Chiranjeevi in the '80s.

By the '90s, he had become 'Megastar' Chiranjeevi. All his roles were about him being the 'Hero' we know today. He was by then the undisputed box office king. In Tamil Nadu, a Rajnikanth had a Kamal Hassan to offer the audience the 'Hero' and the 'Actor'. Hindi cinema had its commercial Heroes, as well as a thriving parallel cinema with actors like Naseeruddin Shah and Om Puri.

But all Telugu films had then was Chiranjeevi – both Hero and Actor. After the '80s, the Hero took over. The roles of the '90s were 'Big' – he played the role of a union leader, a professor, the leader of an auto-rickshaw union, the protective elder brother. He had some of the biggest blockbusters, and the numbers he raked in were unparalleled, especially for an industry that barely spilled beyond its geographical boundaries. Despite this, he also had some big flops, which nearly derailed his political launch.

The film that got him back on track was *Indra*, released in 2002. It was associated with a popular anecdote, a story Telugu people want to believe, making it worth telling. In one scene in the film, the protagonist returns to his hometown after years. He's stayed away from his home, his people, his food, the colours and the soil. He has missed them and is probably worried that the people have forgotten him. But when he steps down from a helicopter, there are tens of thousands of people waiting to see him. They go berserk, like they have even seen God. Indra, moved and touched, goes down and kisses the red soil. There are tears in his eyes. As he heads back home, the tens of thousands have multiplied to become lakhs of people. Entire towns have come to a standstill just to see him.

All of this make for great visuals. And they would have been a great cinematic achievement had the people been paid extras.

Except they were not.

These were people who had gathered for the love of Chiranjeevi. For the entire sequence, Chiranjeevi was not Indra but himself – showered with adoration. The audience, too, saw Chiranjeevi the megastar. Like his character Indra, Chiranjeevi may have wondered whether he was forgotten since he hadn't had an industry-shaking blockbuster in a decade. Yet, people turned up. In lakhs.

Six years later, after doing multiple films that portrayed Chiranjeevi as a mass saviour, he forayed into politics with his Praja Rajyam Party.

On-screen, he was a Telugu megastar; in politics, he was Chiranjeevi – the politician from the Kapu caste. Perhaps this is when the Kapus first felt that it was their 'turn' to control the state. The Kammas had NTR The Reddys have always had power and had a successful ruler in Y.S.R., and now, if the Kapus – historically aligned with the Reddys or Kammas – got behind Telugu cinema's most popular star, they could succeed.

They didn't.

Chiranjeevi could barely hold ground on real political issues. His populist moves seemed meek compared to the ones promised by Y.S.R, who was then the incumbent chief minister. Crowds were more eager to see him as the 'star' than listen to him talk about how he would save the state. For someone so used to being the most respected man in the industry, being a politician seemed almost ill-suited for Chiranjeevi: in his new avatar, his image was tarnished and he was constantly abused and disrespected by local political officials. At some point, when he wasn't served coffee, Chiranjeevi lost his temper at a local party worker; the worker yelled back at him.

The man who kissed the earth, while being cheered by thousands was now being humiliated over a cup of coffee. Then came the final blow: the accusation that he and his brother-in-law, Allu Aravind, were 'auctioning' MLA tickets to the highest bidder behind the scenes, especially Kapus. It's a practice associated with all political parties, but with Chiranjeevi, it was different, because he had been put on a pedestal and then turned out to be the same as everyone else. Chiranjeevi's logic may have been that if he was going to be voted into power, he might as well make money to run the party.

In the 2009 elections, the party won only eighteen out of 294 Assembly seats and zero seats to the Parliament. Chiranjeevi lost his seat in his own hometown of Paalakollu. By the end of the journey, even the Kapus weren't sure if he was the right person, causing a split in the vote bank. In 2011, Chiranjeevi merged Praja Rajyam Party with the Congress.

Eventually, he returned to films in 2017. Those films have raked in blockbuster numbers, but it just isn't the same any more. It's tough to believe him when he saves people now. He has scored a political 'own goal', and that's all people see on the scoresheet. As someone who's played a goalkeeper, he would know that better than anyone else.

The current biggest political and Telugu film icon, Pawan Kalyan, Chiranjeevi's brother, has his own party, Janasena Party. Kalyan, too, is technically Kapu. However, he has publicly stated that he doesn't need the support of any particular caste. He wants to be viewed as a pan-caste figure. Having failed to find the perfect allegiance with the

Reddys and Kammas, the Kapus have also failed to produce and rally behind one cinema Hero who could put them on the political map and tilt things in their favour. The Erra cinema of the '80s and '90s and R. Narayana Murthy helped traditionally disenfranchised castes find legitimacy in the popular imagination, while other dominant castes succeeded politically and economically. The Kapus slipped through the cracks – like the middle child.

The Killer: One Stab for All

There's a dead body in front of us. Thank god, it's not real. Four suspects. There could be more.

The Brahmins had found a director in K. Vishwanath, who made great sensitive films that had rounded protagonists. Before Karan Johar gave Bollywood his version of melodramatic blockbuster 'K' films, K. Vishwanath gave the Telugu film industry his own brand of classics in 'S' films: *Swarnakamlam* (The Golden Lotus), *Sagara Sangamam* (Confluence of the Seas) and his most famous work *Sankarabharanam*, named after the raaga in Carnatic music. Like with curd rice, his films are best enjoyed on lazy afternoons with families.

If the women in his films danced, it was because they enjoyed it, or at least they danced gracefully without just becoming objects of heterosexual fantasy. The men were manly, but not hypermasculine. The elderly were respected, but also challenged. The young were given wings, but also made to reflect upon their actions. There were songs, but they seemed woven into the story rather than thrust on the audience to titillate them. To date, young actors rue the lack of a director of his calibre. K. Vishwanath has raked in multiple awards. His film *Swati Mutyam* (The White Pearl) is the only film from the Telugu film industry that has been sent for Oscar nominations from India.

Regardless, it is impossible to ignore the Brahmanical lens of Vishwanath's cinema. The essence is always this: 'The times maybe changing, but without Brahmins, there is no culture.' While Brahmins lost their political importance, like the strokes underneath a signature, K. Vishwanath gave the caste a cultural flourish in the '70s and '80s.

The Rajus also found a Hero in Prabhas, the lead of the film *Baahubali* that shot him to global fame. His uncle, Krishanam Raju, was a politician. Prabhas carries the legacy of the Raju caste, which claims to have hailed from a lineage of kings. Prabhas' recent films have subtle mentions of his royal lineage. In *Baahubali*, he plays a king. There is a line in the film that reiterates the position of his caste: '*Vaadekkadunna Raje*. (Wherever he may be, he shall remain a king/ Raju.)' Even in his action thriller *Saaho* (Let Victory Be Yours), in which he plays a thief and the heir to a mafia don, there are references to how he is a king. In the end, he distributes his money for social-welfare schemes. It's a terribly awkward fit: the man is a cold-blooded murderer, an action hero who jumps off buildings over hundred stories high … and yet he reminds audience of his caste.

There are suspects beyond castes too. Tamil cinema and Marathi cinema, for instance, have found in Pa. Ranjith and Nagaraj Manjule, respectively as credible Dalit voices. Even when R. Narayana Murthy wants to tell the story of Dalits and Adivasis, it just isn't the same as having a Dalit and Adivasi filmmaker or Hero narrate their own stories. Moreover, by his own admission, the multiplex revolution too contributed to his films being flushed out of the system. In the time of single screens, R. Narayana Murthy's films attracted tremendous crowds – each one a celebration. Like fresh breath after eating a mint, each song in his film lingered in the mouth of his audience. People would come from the villages in autos, tractors and bullock carts just to watch his films.

Times are different now. Single screens are far fewer, if non-existent. Multiplexes attract the rich and are suspicious of the poor; fans have been replaced by air conditioning, and another type of fan has been replaced by an audience member who might be more upset by bad popcorn than a bad film.

Imagine watching *Erra Sainyan* now. In a multiplex. I would walk into a theatre with popcorn that's over-salted, over-caramelized, over-buttered. I would stand up for the national anthem, displaying an adequate amount of patriotism, lest I be accused of anti-nationalism by hawks with patriot-meters.

The film would begin. Red screen. Red font.

Erra Sainyam.

Credits roll. The R. Narayna Murthy show begins. People would probably scoff at how outdated his acting style is. Comments would be passed on the terrible camera work. *Weak cinematography* – as we all tut.

The same plot. Sister. Warden. Sister gets married to her rapist. Audience would rightly wince at this. It would make sense to nobody in the audience. As of these things have happened only in these sorts of films and never had an iota of truth. Nobody would relate to the issue. R. Narayana Murthy would sing about Koyas, Gonds, Konda Reddys – tribes that share the forest. Names that barely ring a bell in multiplexes. Sometime later, he's thrown out of his land. The acting would seem melodramatic, not realistic enough. Would anybody actually react like this?

The popcorn would probably have run out at this point. Hands icky with salt and butter and whatever goes into caramel popcorn; patience running thin.

When the police officer turns his back on R. Narayana Murthy, when the righteous lawyer loses hope and encourages the tribes to take up arms, the lack of 'grey' in the characters would be dissected. Not grey enough – far too preachy and unrealistic. The characters are too black and white. When the communist flag floats through the sky – the zamindars are terrified of it; R. Narayana Murthy and his tribe members worshipping it – the scene could be compared to

The Gods Must Be Crazy, a film in which a tribe ends up worshipping a glass bottle because they have never encountered such a hard substance. These filmmakers can't even be original, people in the multiplex might grumble.

How much longer for the second filling of the popcorn?

The interval would come. Folks would be relieved. Curse the long lines. Popcorn. Cola. Curse them for not having change. Card payment. Restroom. Back in the seat.

Back in the lives of the tribe, R. Narayana Murthy and a band of men and women have taken up arms and become Naxalites. Maybe we would laugh at the irony that the Hero is a Naxalite, but we all stood up for the national anthem sometime back. The police begin to crush the revolt. Even children on-screen are not spared and are subjected to utmost brutality. Food and water supplies are cut off for the group. And then comes the scene that would make the entire theatre regret the food and drinks.

A wounded Naxalite needs water, and the water supplies are blocked by the police, an aged member takes out a pot and places a towel on top of it – a red towel. He lifts a fistful of brown soil and pours it on top of the red cloth.

The aged man and the other Naxalites collectively urinate into the pot. The cloth and the soil filter out the urine to give pure water that percolates inside the pot. They make the fallen Naxalite drink that water, and he feels better. Everything in the forest has an answer. Trees. Land. Guns. Ideology. Even your own piss. It's a powerful message. But the modern audience would find this as an assault on their senses, especially the ones who found the urinals of the multiplex too smelly.

Later in the film, R. Narayana Murthy's son is killed by the police officers. It's all over, people would complain. But many in the multiplex wouldn't know the son is named after Komaram Bheem, the Gond tribal leader who led a revolt against an authoritarian regime. It's metaphor for how the biggest leaders of the tribes have been mercilessly killed by members of the non-tribes. So, when R. Narayana Murthy and his band of Naxalites continue the fight after Bheem's death, it is a message to continue the fight against oppressive forces. But there's a good chance that message would be lost in a multiplex.

The upcoming film by Rajamouli, *RRR*, seems to have a character inspired by Komaram Bheem but anyone who follows the director's work would be willing to bet all their money that the Komaram Bheem that inspires R. Narayana Murthy's films and countless Adivasis would be different from the action hero that Rajamouli will present.

When the film finally ends with the Naxalites, villagers, men, women, children, the aged and even the reformed police officers uniting against the oppressive zamindar, the climax would be far too simplistic. In a multiplex, the audience might not fully comprehend how powerful it is when the members of the tribe reject everything the zamindar stood for – the 'land' documents that the state imposed on them and the money that they don't have and because of which they are rendered poor. The weapons in there are hands are crowbars, sickles, hammers, guns, ploughs, anger and unity. In the final shot of the film, R. Narayana Murthy lifts the hand of the dead zamindar who has fallen on the ground. It's odd. The villain is dead and R. Narayana Murthy has had his revenge. But the film isn't over; he squeezes one more moment – a Hero moment.

The fist of the zamindar has some soil within it, and R. Narayana Murthy squeezes it out of the dead man's palm. The oppressive zamindar might be buried in the ground, but he will take none of the soil with him. The soil is for the tribe; they own it. In a multiplex, this moment would perhaps fail to cause too many goosebumps; but in a single-screen theatre, the scene would have been received exactly the way it was intended.

Erra Sainyam doesn't end with 'The End' or the more Telugu '*Shubham* (May Good Luck Be with You)' card. If it did, it wouldn't be Erra cinema. The film ends with a card that says: *Bhoovimukthi poratalu varthillali*. Long Live the Protests for Land Liberation!

Walking out of the theatre, the multiplex audience would probably be feeling guilty on two accounts – first, at being so helpless at the plight of tribes so 'far' away; second, for wanting to watch a simple and more straightforward film.

I could be wrong. In theory, the multiplex audience could be kinder to the film than I give them credit for. But there is one person I know – who fits the multiplex audience stereotype – who would never appreciate the film. After trawling through Facebook, I managed to find DK after nearly two decades. He is obviously older – thick moustache, tall. He hasn't grown up to be a boxer like he promised me he would. He probably would accuse me of not having married Cherry like I promised him I would. The inhaler is absent, but it has been replaced with a prop – shades that manage to creep into all his photos. Like a Telugu Hero. More importantly, he is extremely proud of his caste; he has shared multiple articles on the topic. He has especially become a fan of one Telugu hero who coincidentally is from the same caste as him. He also supports the political party that is known to support his own caste. The colour of Erra cinema would directly go against the colours of the party he supports. He believes good days can come for his caste only if the Hero and the party join hands.

He wouldn't accept my friend request on Facebook. Well … I can't be sure as I haven't sent him one. Perhaps all these suspects have killed our friendship too. It's understandable. How could the people stand a chance if even *People's Star* can be killed?

5

Fans: Rebels, Dealers, Fathers

'Because the fact of the matter is that although individual revolutionaries succeeded, the revolution failed.'
—*Easy tigers, Raging Bulls*

FADE IN
EXT. SCHOOL –ENCH - DAY

Twelve-year-old Krishna is sitting on a bench, writing a letter, as a group of boys behind him play cricket. He is shorter than the other boys, as well as darker and more rotund.

'Dear Father, it's been ten days since I've come to this hostel. I hate it.'

He pauses before he writes more. Two big and menacing boys walk up to him.

BULLY ONE
Do you want to be called a fatty?

BULLY TWO
Do you want to be called a blackie?
KRISHNA
Call me Krishna.

Krishna swallows air. The bullies see the letter. Krishna tries to hide it under his shirt, but the bigger bully holds him by the shoulders and pins him on the bench. The other bully snatches the letter and tears it into pieces. The bullies laugh and leave.

Krishna sits on the stone bench and begins to cry before removing another blank paper from his pant pocket.

FADE OUT

All Irrationalities Are Equal

You probably laughed the last time you saw him. Pouring milk over a giant cut-out of a South Indian star, while a journalist looks on, amused. *This bloody young man wasting his time*, is how audience chastised the fan from behind the television screen. Like dopamine, superiority complex kicked into your head. *My life is surely devoted to more meaningful activities than that.* He was probably the butt of the joke when talking to your friends about the crazy things people do for Heroes. You've even laughed at the star he adores, for looking comical when delivering punchlines and dancing awkwardly to a folk tune. *It's all so silly – this whole charade of being a 'fan'.*

Of course, admiration is part human nature, serving the rational purpose of fuelling ambitions. A young batsman will imitate the shots played by Sachin Tendulkar; an aspiring actor will dissect the performance of every Oscar winner; a poet will tear into the lyrical qualities of *Howl* by Allen Ginsberg. All of this is 'rational' behaviour.

At the heart of being amused by the South Indian cinema fan, then, is the question about purpose: Why? Why on earth would you do that? The fan of the Telugu Hero seems doubly irrational. While other fans are loyal to individual actors and stars, fans of the Telugu Heroes are also fans of the family their favourite stars belong to. They will rally behind stars who are sons, grandsons, brothers, brothers-in-law, nephews of the Hero they worship. The fans in other film industries root for an individual Hero, but fans of the Telugu cinema support entire families. They firmly stand behind the Hero's family through thick and thin, and the concern of nepotism is brushed away by the idea that some families just have 'it'. This logic dictates that if the actors who belong to the first families of the industry didn't have the required talent to be actors, stars and Heroes, they would be punished by regular film-going audience.

But what makes a fan go crazy for a Hero? Why would he pour milk over an actor's cut-out? Why would he stand in a queue outside theatres to catch a film, if it isn't for the acting chops? Why would he be so madly in love with a film star? What makes someone want to abuse strangers online when they criticize the star he adores? What makes someone submit themselves to another human being, not in servitude but in awe? There could be many historical explanations. One could use the argument that the religious forces in the sub-continent have inspired bhakti (devotion) and that this must be a genetic remnant of that culture. Those who were once devoted to gods find their spiritual descendants worshipping at the altar of the men in the moving images. But this argument would strip these fans of their 'present' condition. Can the devotion of Tulsidas to Ram be compared to a fan who throws papers up in the air in jubilation when his favourite Hero walks on screen? This claim, while appealing in providing rationality through history and myth, doesn't use the socio-personal causes that lead a fan to worship a hero. Maybe it's a mutation of the patron-client relationship that is popular in rural India – a rich or an upper-caste man who has a coterie of men who are loyal to him and his family and their subsequent generations share a similar bond. That too doesn't hold because in this case most Heroes are barely aware of the existence of the individual fans and their personal lives. To the Hero, the 'fans' are a monolith.

How do we understand fans then? By simply talking to them. *What are their lives like beyond the Hero? What pushed them off the rational edge? What invisible force ensures that their heads never bob back up? How do we choose from the thousands of fans who drive and maintain a Hero's image and stardom?* Suppose this was a maths problem – one of those probability questions where blue balls and red balls were hidden in socks, and we were expected to guess the colour of a ball picked at random. Let's imagine all the fans of all the Telugu Heroes stuffed into a giant sock, each hanging on to the gridded threads like grabbing the rungs of a ladder. Suppose you had to pick at random from this gargantuan sock. In this sock, there would mostly be male fans, usually between eighteen and thirty. In terms of their economic range, they would fall between middle class to poor. There are exceptions, but these are not unreasonable assumptions to make before picking fans from inside the sock. I put my hand into the sock and outcome M and B – two fans of the Telugu Heroes who exist in a world where their irrationality is different from other irrationalities.

CUT TO:
INT. SINGLE-SCREEN THEATRE, A SMALL TOWN
IN ANDHRA PRADESH, NIGHT

A group of young boys sit in the front row as a Telugu film plays. They nervously look around to see if anyone from their boarding school is there to catch them. Krishna is amongst them. The film is *Mosagallaki Mosagadu* (The Cheater of Cheaters), a cheap rip-off of *Makenna's Gold*. Coincidentally, the name of the Hero in the film is also Krishna.

BOY ONE
Krishna, look, the Hero's name is also Krishna.

For the first time in his boarding school life, Krishna notices that he is not called 'fatty' or 'blackie'. The boy then proceeds to put a hand around Krishna's shoulder as they watch the film. Krishna smiles for the first time since joining school.

Later, he stands on his seat, touches his middle finger to his thumb, and whistles for the first time. Krishna has a new favourite Hero, with whom he shares a name.

Cut to:

The Rebel Who Grew Ginger

Bhagat Singh. That's who this is really about for M. How far are you willing to go to see something you really want to see? How far are you willing to go to experience something that seems beyond your reach? What if it cost you money? (It will.) What if it cost you time? (That too.) But what if this experience also cost you your truths? What if you had to alter your sense of reality to get what you really wanted? Would you do it? Everyone would laugh at you, jeer at you, call you insane … nobody would get it.

And yet, for a few fleeting moments, you get to experience what you really want – something grand.

Remember all of this, because it will come up later.

But when I first talk to M, it begins with the song *Closer* by The Chainsmokers. That was M's caller tune when I call him.

Hey, I was doing just fine before I met you
I drink too much
And that's an issue, but I'm okay.

I admire his WhatsApp display picture of a heart-shaped cactus in a red pot as the song continues to play. It has the quality of a photo taken by an amateur photographer as opposed to the ones of plants reserved for glossy wildlife magazines.

We ain't getting older
We ain't getting older
We ain't getting older

Before the lyrics can go to the next verse, he picks up the phone and agrees to meet me.

Let me begin with a confession: I don't know why M is someone you must know about. You could ignore him if you saw him on the road sitting in an autorickshaw next to the driver. Or if he was standing in line at a fast-food chain memorizing the correct pronunciation of Mayonnaise – one of those words that requires him to sculpt his mouth in awkward ways before he can get the accurate pronunciation – you might decide to help him arrive at the correct intonation or be annoyed because you were caught behind 'someone like him'. These are experiences he's faced before, M admits.

He also looks a little older than his actual age. It's been pointed out to him more often than he likes to hear it. But that's not the worst he's heard; he's also constantly reminded about how he is stouter than average twenty-year olds. His friends make fun of his below average-height. And relatives mock him for the colour of his skin – something he's already underconfident about. His parents have taken on the responsibility of reminding him about his dwindling grades in college, an institution he loathes for its mediocre faculty. But none of these are things he wants to be remembered by, despite being constantly reminded that he's a sum of these things.

He knows he's better.

This is how much M tells me on the phone. He says I need to meet him to talk about the two things he wants to be remembered by. The first one is that he's a 'big fan' of the Telugu Hero Pawan Kalyan. The second is love for horticulture and the nursery owned by his father.

That's why the photo of a heart-shaped cactus in his display picture.

He asks me to meet him in person at the nursery, which is on the edges of Hyderabad off a highway leading to Mumbai. I bring up the cactus, and he tells me it's called *hoya kerri* – a Southeast Asian variant popular in Europe as a Valentine's Day gift. Before I can prod further, he shyly admits that he's waiting to one day gift it to a woman who falls in love with him. The nursery has rows of potted plants with green leaves, like a low hanging green gaseous cloud covering the arid red soil underneath our feet. Some of the younger plants are sheltered under a green cloth.

He tells me he needs to be at the nursery as part of his regular visits to check on the new batch of plants. There aren't too many others in the nursery – a helper who tends to the plants during the day and a security guard at the entrance. Other than that, it's just the two of us and hundred different species of plants witnesses to M's love for the actor-politician Pawan Kalyan.

M first tells me the real reason he wanted to meet in the nursery: if he discusses his love for an actor in any other public place, he faces judgemental looks. He feels most comfortable in the nursery. He doesn't even wait for me to ask the first question I had prepared regarding what it means to be a 'fan'. Like a hungry child, he gobbles up the opportunity to talk about his favourite star. 'I actually became a fan of him after he started his political party.' Pawan Kalyan launched his Jana Sena Party prior to the 2014 elections. Although he didn't contest, he promised to be a gatekeeper of good politics. He lent his support to the BJP and the TDP and aggressively took part in a campaign whose slogan was '*Congress Hatao, Desh Bachao* (Remove the Congress, Save the Nation)'.

'I used to watch his films and loved his style of acting. He is not a great actor, but when he's on-screen it's so much fun. Especially when he gets angry on-screen. It's so much fun. You feel it.'

I ask him what he means.

'When he's on-screen and angry with the government, the villain, or even a comedian … I know he means it. Other people look like they are acting. But when Pawan Kalyan does it, especially when you see him on a big screen with hundreds of other people, it feels like he's trying to talk to my soul.' M breaks into laughter. 'That was a little too dramatic. No?'

I take the liberty to laugh and say, 'A little.'

He buries himself into his phone and extracts a video from one of Pawan Kalyan's films. It's a film titled *Cameraman Gangatho Rambabu* (With Cameraman Ganga, Rambabu). Pawan Kalyan has been lying in an hospital bed, and he decides enough is enough. He walks out and there are hundreds of reporters waiting to hear him talk. An honest reporter, he has picked a bone with an extremist politician who wants to rid society off its non-Telugu elements. Sitting on the steps of the hospital, Pawan Kalyan wants to talk to the people of the state. He looks straight into the camera, his face smeared across the screen. All the television screens in the state are blaring his image. Like a God, Pawan Kalyan has invaded all the houses in the Telugu states. He looks tired, but not physically – tired of the system, of the people, of being helpless and, more importantly, of the people he is addressing. He chastises the people of the state for their apolitical and lazy attitude towards political change, for limiting political discussions as a way to kill time in the evening. Everyone has suggestions for Sachin Tendulkar, Barack Obama, and the United Nations, but no one is looking after their own state. He is sick and tired of them.

Then he finally addresses the people – *YOU!* The people of the state watching him in the film. Those watching the film in the theatres in the Telugu states. People like me watching the video on YouTube. He's riled up now. His hands move about like he's conducting an improvised orchestra and words come out faster than he can process them. That's how angry he is. He asks us if we are really the 'youth'. He asks us why we are so complacent when politicians barter our collective future for their private benefit. He asks why we complain about not having enough time to care for our politics, when we can find the time to talk to girlfriends. He even takes a meta dig where he wonders how the youth finds time to stand in line for hours to buy tickets for their favourite Telugu Hero's film. *Why do you need a Hero? Are you not a hero in your own family?*

Eventually, the 'you' in his speech has narrowed down to young men in the Telugu states, who seemed to be plagued by the disease of cinema and Hero-worship. He wonders why nobody takes personal responsibility before criticizing society for lacking any social responsibility towards one another. He then quotes the Telugu poet Sri Sri, arguing that the following lines were meant for people like 'you'.

Yamukalu Kullina
Vayasalu Mallina
Somarullara Chaavandi

With rotting bones,
And ageing bodies,
All the lazy ones, die.

He proceeds to quote Tilak, the Telugu writer famous for hard hitting prose and poetry.

Devuda Rakshinchu Naa Deshanni
God Please save my nation.

At the peak of his anger, as the monologue reaches its climax, Pawan Kalyan says, 'What can God do if you are like this?'

M stops the video to gauge my reaction. He has clearly seen this hundreds of times and the thrill from each viewing has never diminished. I tell him it's powerful. I mean it.

'Didn't you feel like this is what Bhagat Singh must have been like?'

I tell him I need to think about that.

M takes over. 'I first saw him in Banjara Hills. I don't even remember why I was there. And I felt the people out there giving me strange glances because someone like me can't be seen 'walking' there casually. Plus, who walks in Banjara Hills?' Banjara Hills is one of the most elite neighbourhoods in the city of Hyderabad, home to the wealthy, famous and powerful. 'At that point, I saw a crowd outside a hair salon, talking about Hero Pawan Kalyan who had just arrived. I obviously wanted to see him, so I joined the crowd. Pawan Kalyan took the time to talk to almost all of us who were there. Imagine that. He spoke to all of us. When he saw me, he placed his hand on my shoulder and asked me my name. When I told him my name, and how big a fan of his I was, he asked me to concentrate on my studies. That time, phones were not so common, and I didn't have the presence of mind to take an autograph. But it was special. Seeing a Hero in front of my eyes for the first time.'

We are served sugary chai by the helper, who brings a pause to the conversation.

'He doesn't have to do any of this. He's doing for me. You. Us.'

I ask M what he means.

'He has the best life he can lead as a film star. Why would he leave all of that if he didn't want to do some good? Sometimes I want to tell him, just be on the big screen and forget the people. I mean, who are these people that he wants to serve? Do you know how much TDP and YSRCP paid every voter in the last two elections?'

I shake my head.

'Two thousand rupees in 2014, and five thousand rupees in 2019. He is so naïve; he didn't pay anybody anything. How can someone win an election like that nowadays? I want to tell him, *we aren't good enough*.' The 'we' here being the people of Andhra Pradesh. 'He should just go back to cinema. For his fans.'

I ask M about the nursery and how long he's been working on this.

'Actually, my father owns this. He saw me wasting time on Pawan Kalyan and fan associations. My scores weren't good either. So, he asked me to help him take care of this. Initially I hated it, but now I see my friends working these night-duty jobs – boring jobs – and I think my life is a lot better. My father makes me go to Pune every month to buy new plants, and I come here three or four times a week to check on things. It's better than being stuck in front of a computer all day.' He picks up his teacup and pours the tea into the red soil underneath us. 'This tea is shit.' He orders for some better tea. 'I would have loved to study History,' M continues. 'Study about freedom fighters. India. But my parents obviously wanted me to get a software job. When I said no, we settled for the middle path – a BCom degree.' He laughs, mulling over how his family arrived at that conclusion. 'What did you study?'

'I did my masters in development studies,' I tell him. He's puzzled by this degree, so I break it down. 'It's like economics without the maths.'

'Your parents allowed you to take it?'

'Not really. I had to fight, but eventually agreed.'

'So you fought against them? Parents want … IAS, IPS…' He bursts out laughing and has clearly amused himself. It's a reference to the Telugu film *Nuvvu Naaku Nacchav* (I Like You), where the protagonist initially wants a big and respectable job – like an IAS or an IPS officer, but eventually settles for any job that pays. 'You had to do a Bhagat Singh in your own family then.'

'What is this obsession with Bhagat Singh?'

'I want to do something for this country. I want people to think I did more than what was expected of me. I don't want to be the guy who only listens. First listened to his father, then his teachers, then his boss. It'll be nice to be like Bhagat Singh. A young person who fought for his country – brave, an inspiration to all young people. I mean look at us now. I'm happy in my nursery. I can't fight against my own parents. You're writing a book about the Telugu cinema. We're all so obsessed with cinema. We don't have that kind of bravery anymore. That's why Pawan Kalyan is important. He fought against his own family to serve the people. His own brother.' He pauses to catch a breath after his rant.

After the debacle of Chiranjeevi's political stint, which ended in him merging his party with the Congress Party, there was speculation about a rift between Pawan Kalyan and Chiranjeevi over the former starting a new political party. It was supposedly against Chiranjeevi's wishes. However, all of this has been hearsay, and nothing has been confirmed.

'That's why when Pawan Kalyan called us for the *kavathu* (March), I went for it. There were lakhs of people in Rajamundhry. He called us all. We were there in lakhs.' On 15 October 2018, the leader of Jana Sena Party called all party cadre and fans to conduct a march as a show of strength across the Godavari Barrage in Rajamundry. Over four lakh people were supposed to have turned up at the event called Praja Porata Yatra (The March of the Struggle for People). 'It was there that all of us saw him next.'

'Who is all of you?' I ask him.

Fresh tea is served, and this time it's much better. It has ginger in it.

'All of my friends.' He notices that I like this tea more. 'That ginger in the tea grows here. If you are interviewing me, I should at least give you good tea. Come, I'll show it to you.'

By the time I ask my next question, he is giving me a tour of the nursery. 'Are all of your friends also Pawan Kalyan fans?'

We reach a small plot. Ginger plants that scrape our knees and thighs are growing in moist soil. 'This ginger is really difficult to grow. My father was against me growing it, but I just wanted to try.'

'I guess you're also a Bhagat Singh then.'

He laughs for a brief moment, but the smile fades. 'Actually ... I met most of my friends because we were part of a Pawan Kalyan fan association. Before I came to Hyderabad, I grew up in Rajamundry. I didn't have too many friends so I joined a local fan association of Pawan Kalyan. We used to take money from home and pool it all in.

If it was Sir's [Pawan Kalyan's] birthday or a new film was releasing, we would order a cake, cut it, and make banners and paste them across town.'

'Why?' I try to avoid the tone of ridicule, but I doubt I was successful.

'It was fun. We did it to celebrate. I mean … what else could I have done in Rajamundry? I used to play cricket, I went to school and junior college, and then I celebrated Pawan Kalyan as a fan.'

'Did your parents know how you were spending the money?'

'They did. They kept yelling at me. They yell even now. But my father was also a big fan of Chiranjeevi when he was young. Even my grandfather was a big fan of Akkineni Nageshwar Rao (ANR). So I guess it's in the genes.'

We reach a section of plants that have giant leaves with the yellows losing a war against the greens. 'This is how we make most of our money. This is the money plant that everyone wants to buy, because it is good for decoration. You see that bamboo plot over there? That's where we grow the lucky bamboo that people use as gifts. It's so much money.' He then takes me to see the flowers in the nursery. Roses in all colours – red, white, yellow, pink, orange. He shows petunias in violet and maroon. Marigolds in flaming yellows and burning orange. There are corn-coloured lilies, jam-coloured ones, and lilies the colour of frost. He cuts lilies with white petals and violet insides, and makes me smell them. 'No lilies smell as good as the ones in my nursery. I can guarantee you. Can you smell it?'

I nod. It's a lie. I can't smell them, and it's probably because I have a blocked nose. But he's convinced of their superior fragrance.

'You know … other Heroes have fans who come from their own castes. They are richer so they make bigger banners. But Pawan Kalyan's fans are from different backgrounds. I'm not from his caste. I have friends who are not even Hindu who still love him. They are from different towns. He really is different from everyone else.'

'Why do you think he lost in the 2019 elections?' Pawan Kalyan contested in two constituencies and lost in both.

'He is too good for the people. We don't deserve him. Back in the day, people thought Bhagat Singh was stupid. But now, we discuss him as much as we discuss Gandhi. One day, people of AP [Andhra Pradesh] will realize what they lost in him.'

I ask him if he's excited that Pawan Kalyan, after supposed retirement from films, is making a comeback by signing nearly four films.

'Yes. Very much. We are already collecting funds to make the biggest banners across Hyderabad. This time, we have money. This time, I'm going to tie the biggest banner we can find.'

'Are you excited about the film?' The first film to release in this series is called *Vakeel Saab* (Lawyer Sir), a remake of the 2016 film *Pink* starring Taapsee Pannu and Amitabh Bachchan, with Pawan Kalyan reprising the role of the latter.

'I am. He's going to play a lawyer. It'll have an impact.' He opens his phone and shows me a WhatsApp group. The group is called 'PK Soldiers'. He scrolls through photoshopped images of Pawan Kalyan as a lion, as Che Guevara, sitting in the chief minister's chair … until he stops at one and hands me the phone. There are images of two men next to each other. The text underneath the photos reads, 'He was hanged by the British. But his revolutionary spirit hasn't died. Now it comes back on screen as *Vakeel Saab*.'

One of the men – the *Vakeel Saab* – is Pawan Kalyan. You know who the other person is.

FADE IN
INT. SINGLE SCREEN THEATRE – DAY

Krishna and his friends are watching another film of actor Krishna. This time, it is the biopic of Alluri Seeta Rama Raju, the Telugu revolutionary who fought against the British by leading multiple tribes in Andhra Pradesh.

Krishna sits in the centre, surrounded by his friends. They are not nervous about being caught any more. They are older, bigger, and have faint moustaches around their lips. On-srceen, actor Krishna bellows as he is shot by British soldiers.

ACTOR KRISHNA
Rutherford, if one Seeta Rama Raju dies,
a hundred thousand shall take his place.
Each one shall become a revolutionary and shake
the foundations of the British Empire.

The theatre erupts. Hundreds of coloured paper, coins and shirts obstruct the projection. Krishna has stood up, whistling and jumping, while standing on his seat. He turns to his friend, the boy who put his arm around him a few years earlier.

KRISHNA
Can your NTR do this to a theatre?
It's been hundred days.
Listen to the sound.

Krishna goes back to whistling at his namesake on-screen.
CUT TO

The Dealer Who Got the Jackpot

If you've ever played amateur poker, there is only one job everyone hates – the dealing. It's like being told the benefits of broccoli after skydiving off a plane. One of the benefits of playing professional poker is that a player never has to perform the menial task of shuffling the cards, dealing them or, worse, hearing complaints about the terrible cards that are being dealt. And yet, no poker table or casino can function without a dealer. A casino can exist with bad gamblers and lucky ones, but it needs a good dealer. Someone smart and affable, someone who loves the job, and someone who is loyal to the owners of the casino. A good dealer will never cheat the owners off their money and will never become a gambler at the casino they serve.

B is one such dealer; except, instead of cards he deals film scripts; gamblers are replaced by producers, directors and struggling actors; luck, as always, remains the same. He asks me to meet him in Krishna Nagar in Hyderabad. It's the casino of dreams and the graveyard of hope – almost every person you meet in Krishna Nagar is gambling away talent, time and bodies at tables that are clearly rigged in favour of the owners of the casino. The 'owners' are not shady mafia bosses who wouldn't mind breaking a leg or bashing a skull if a debt is not paid; they are the Telugu Heroes, who control the dream that cinema sells. They sell the dream that if you go all in, at some point, you win the jackpot. They sell the idea that you are tantalizingly close to the dream, just one role away, one extra night on a couch in a producer's favourite hotel, one more year before you resign yourself to that job you despise, then all of what you go through emotionally and physically becomes worth it. Conversations in Krishna Nagar's tea-and-snack shops are buzzing with notes about upcoming auditions, affairs of directors and producers and actors, costume shops that give discounts, choreographers who fondle young boys once dance rehearsals are finished. Each city with a thriving film industry has one of these 'casinos'. Chennai has Kodambakkam, Mumbai has Andheri West. Krishna Nagar looks punishingly ordinary from the outside. Roads under construction, buildings that can only flex a few storeys, open drains, bakeries with aged egg puffs, and bars with dying livers. Krishna Nagar is close to Jubilee Hills and Banjara Hills, which are synonymous with wealth, fame, and power – where the owners of the casino live.

The location B sends me over WhatsApp is that of a popular Biriyani joint in Krishna Nagar. It's an odd place for him to ask me to meet him. Krishna Nagar is where strugglers congregate, not fans. Besides B is no 'ordinary' fan. He manages an actor who is related to his favourite actor – Chiranjeevi. He is a 'Mega' Loyal fan, the word 'Mega' also playing on actor Chiranjeevi's title as 'Mega Star'. I'm late for the meeting and the heat punishes me like a schoolteacher punishes a truant child. From the Biriyani joint, B makes me walk about half a kilometre to reach his office, ensuring I cut across the belly of Krishna Nagar with its smell of biriyani and sewage.

Once inside his office, it's a ten-minute wait before he meets me. It begins with a complaint. An important part of his job is to listen to stories from directors to filter them before the actor he manages lends an ear. There are some excellent stories, but some terrible ones too. He is still unsure which category the one he just heard before me falls into. In his forties, short, dark and with a moustache that fences his upper lip, B has outgrown his hair in the front to cover the receding hairline clawing at his scalp. Like coffee mug stains on a white desk, dark circles underneath his eyes define his face. He sits opposite me in a plush office chair, like the ones you would find in a corporate office. The table I sit at is where many aspiring filmmakers and writers have waged bets on their scripts – most unsuccessfully.

B places his phone on the brown table that separates us and jumps straight into the topic. Like with most people who fall in love with the Telugu films, it began with a Chiranjeevi film in the '80s. His dad took him for the film *Khaidi* (Prisoner). The film is inspired from *Rambo: First Blood*, but localized through a class and caste conflict in a small village in Andhra Pradesh. B was baptized in a small theatre in Vizag, where he saw the film with his father – one of his earliest and most pleasant memories with his father.

'My father was a big fan of watching films in theatres. Once I was born, he didn't want to stop the habit. So, he used to take me to theatres. Even now, we mostly just talk about films. What else do fathers and sons talk about in this country?' He laughs. 'As I grew older, even I started to love watching Chiranjeevi on the big screen. There is something about him; you could say he puts you in a trance.'

'Did you want to be an actor? Most people who watch films want—'

'Not really. I just wanted to be as close to him as possible. I would do anything for that experience. Back then, we didn't have online booking [of tickets], right? I'm talking about the '80s. If a Chiranjeevi film was releasing the next day, we used to stay at a mutual friend's house.'

'We?'

'All my friends. We were all fans of Chiranjeevi. We used to stay in a friend's house and leave around 2 in the morning, heading for the ticket counter. We used to ride our cycles and stand in line at the theatre for hours, just so that we could get tickets on time.'

'At 2 a.m.?'

'This is nothing. There were folks who used to come be there by 12. I don't think they even went to sleep. It's how people buy iPhones now. We set the trend before it became a trend.' He breaks into laughter. This is a reference to a dialogue in a Pawan Kalyan film. 'Those fans who used to turn up earlier were bigger fans than us.'

'What do you mean?'

He gets a call on his phone before he can answer. It's from one of the Telugu film industry's most sought-after producers. B looks at me apologetically because this is a call he must attend to. He picks it up and walks out of the room, but he is within hearing distance. Like a thief robbing a bank, his voice changes at 'hello'. B tells the producer that the story he heard might not suit the Hero. Unlike others, this Hero does not lie about the dates, B says, and he promises the producer that, while he is definitely interested in the idea, it's important that the Hero suit the film and the producer make money. It's about maintaining a personal relationship with the producer. The conversation swiftly proceeds to final pleasantries before B cuts the call. The film whose narration B heard before he met me will not get made. Or at least B and the hero he manages won't be a part of it.

He comes back and takes his seat. 'Sorry. This will keep happening. Please don't mind. So, those fans were crazy. These days a film's success is measured in crores of rupees at a box office. Back in the '80s, in Vizag and the rest of Andhra Pradesh, they used to measure a film's success by number of days and number of centres. So, if a Krishna film played for hundred days in fifty centres, Chiranjeevi fans used to try and make their film play for hundred days in seventy-five centres.'

Krishna is the former actor 'Super Star' Krishna, with whom Chiranjeevi shared a brief rivalry in the '80s before ascending the throne as the 'king' of the box office. Before I can ask B what he means by 'make the film play', he answers the question.

'They used to buy hundreds of tickets. Spend all their money that they used to get from home. It was worse than what people do now. In fact, I think this is better.'

He is referring to the current trend amongst fans of South Indian Heroes where they trend hashtags for birthdays and film's first looks on Twitter or likes and views on YouTube. They range from the simple #HappyBirthdayAlluArjun to honour the birthday of their favourite star to #InsurgentBheemNTR to celebrate the character played by a Hero in the next film. These Twitter trends and posts reach figures of hundreds of thousands to millions. Along the way there are accusations of paid posts, multiple accounts by fans to spike numbers up, public relations officers (PROs) of Heroes engaging in social media 'warfare'. A similar game is played on YouTube. Meanwhile fans trend lewd hashtags meant to denigrate the rival of their favourite Hero. Sometimes, even the children of their favourite Heroes get birthday wishes reaching hundreds of thousands. The idea is to make the presence of a Hero's fandom felt on social media.

B continues. 'At least now they are only wasting time online. Before, they used to waste their family savings.'

What about the vitriol that so many people – blue ticks and the common netizens alike – face because of opinions that are shared against Heroes. There's misogyny, death threats, verbal abuse, hounding across social media platforms, leaking of private information of non-consenting parties. I ask him if Heroes can control their fans and demand them to not take part in such activities.

'Fans have to be willing to listen. They are not. Again, you have to understand that before this, fans used to fight – *physically*. I know two sets of fans who beat each other with hockey sticks and cricket bats because their film dates clashed. One side complained about being allocated bad theatres. One side complained about releasing on a bad date. Even decades earlier, Chiranjeevi fans and Krishna fans used to fight outside theatres. Now, things are better. If someone is willing to go to the extent of fighting till they bleed, what can Heroes do?'

I am unconvinced, but I sense him scrambling for answers, so I move on. I ask him if he ever participated in such activities. His phone rings again; after a quick glance at it, he decides to cut the call. 'I couldn't. In between I was distracted by my studies and career and a software job. So, by the time I could be a *real* fan, I was in the US. I had gone there for work.' He names the software giant he used to work for. 'Even when I was there, I still made sure I watched Chiranjeevi films. Do you know your way around America?'

'Reasonably,' I say.

'I used to drive from Seattle to Detroit over a long weekend to just watch Chiranjeevi films.' Another call interrupts us. This time, I don't catch the name because he answers in a hurry. There is a marked change in tone again. He is more at ease, like talking to a friend on a Sunday afternoon. He tells them the script won't work. *The kid has watched too many Netflix films and has come up with some concept. It won't work.* They exchange a few more details about their lives.

Meanwhile, I Google the distance between Seattle and Detroit to make sense of the distance.

It's 2,349 miles – roughly 3,800 kilometres. In terms of what that travel would mean in India: he would have had to travel from the northern-most city of Leh to Kanyakumari, the southern-most tip of Tamil Nadu. Set to rousing music and picturesque shots of mountains, deserts, forests, villages, and beaches … this is the extent of travel that Indian film male protagonists undertake to understand that the real love of their life was the heroine they left behind. In the decade of 2010–20, the man was usually Ranbir Kapoor, and the woman was often Deepika Padukone. B did this over a weekend in America for a Chiranjeevi film.

After finishing the call, he settles back into his chair. 'So, I drove all the way. It's almost a coast-to-coast journey.' He beams with pride, his moustache like an olive wreath crowning his words. He names the Chiranjeevi film he did it for: *Jai Chiranjeeva* (Hail Chiranjeeva), which released in 2005. The story is about Satyamoorthy (Chiranjeevi), a small-town uncle who loses his niece when an arms dealer fires a bullet at her, while testing a new weapon. To avenge her death, Chiranjeevi decides to kill the villain, who lives across the world in Los Angles. The film was a spectacular flop.

I am so amused by B's grand gesture for Chiranjeevi I am scared my immediate question sounds like I'm mocking him. 'But, why?'

'I just wanted to see a Telugu film. I wanted to see a Chiranjeevi film. It helped that I was single then. In fact, I thought if I drove so far to see the film, I might as well drive a little farther and come back to India.' He giggles at his own joke before regaining composure.

'Anyway, the point I was trying to make was that I really fought as a fan when I was in the US. Have you heard of discussion boards?'

I shake my head. He digs into his phone and extracts old chat messages and tabs of web pages under various headings.

Best Mega Film.

Why Mega Heroes are Better than N Family? (The N family here refers to the descendants of NTR).

Are N family members Chow fans? (Chow is a shortened version of Chowdhary, who are members of the Kamma caste.)

'So we used to fight here. This was like social media before there was social media.'

'What did you guys talk about here?'

'Everything. From films, Heroes, combinations between Heroes and directors, and Heroes and Heroines—'

'Was it polite? Or was it full of abuses like Twitter is now?'

'It had everything. Good, bad, and abuses alike. I used to stay up late in the night and try and fight with other fans defending Chiranjeevi and his films.'

'All of this was in the US?'

'Yes.'

When he speaks of his time in America, it's as if that chapter and geography in his life wouldn't have existed if Chiranjeevi wasn't such a big part of it. That was probably the only proof of him having ever stayed there. Like the black stripes of a tiger, he is only partially successful in hiding the real colour of his time there. The conversation dissolves back into itself.

'Can I ask you something?' I ask. I've been doing this for the last hour or so, yet this next question seems to need special permission.

B looks puzzled and threatened by this wedge in the conversation, like a gambler being asked his opinion before going all-in. 'Yes?'

'What do you really mean when you say you're a fan? Why do you do this for someone?'

He gives me the look often given to me by multiple maths teachers: *I'm going to try one more time before it's not my fault anymore.* He fiddles with his phone. His brain is projecting words and editing them out. He really wants me to understand what he feels and why he thinks a certain way. *Why would you argue with strangers and abuse them over Chiranjeevi's films?* I want to ask. *Why not?* His silence seems to answer. Like a Chess grandmaster, his brain wants to circumvent this stalemate.

'First you need to understand that there is an aura around Chiranjeevi.' It's apparent that my face sinks at this attempt at deification. I want to plaster my face muscles back into their normal position, to an expression that says *I get it.* 'If you ever see him talk to fans, the way he cares about us ... everyone ... the kind of social service he does. He has started blood banks, constantly trying to do something good for the people, the film industry. Nobody does something like that. Nobody needs to do that. He may have failed in politics, but he is a good human being.'

'Do you follow politics closely?'

'I don't. My life is only cinema. I don't like politics, but I want to do good for the society. Give something back.' The phone rings again. This time he cuts the call without glancing. 'I'll tell you one more story. I'm also a big fan of Pawan Kalyan. If Chiranjeevi was like a God to us, then Pawan Kalyan played characters like me. I was in college when he made his debut. I loved him. And I am a big fan of him too. Both in cinema and in politics. Before I met him because of my profession, I got married to this girl who promised she would be comfortable not working and staying at home and taking care of the children. I was very clear about this. Because I grew up as a lonely child. My father wasn't there and even my mother was working. I don't want my children going through the same thing. So I made sure she knew my reasons for asking her to be a housewife. Except, after marriage and having a child, she wanted to go back to work. She didn't want to be a homemaker, and I didn't want my child to be alone at home. There was no way forward, but a divorce. We got one.' He takes me through that journey with a calm, detached tone, as if reciting answers from an examination he already aced. He continues. 'I was a little scared of telling people about this. But then I met Pawan Kalyan. He has married thrice, divorced twice. Never has he shied away from talking about it in public. There is no shame or insecurity associated with it. Instead of staying in an unhappy marriage like most, he chose the path that made him happy. He told everyone the truth. That's what he also told me. "You can't hide the truth or run away from your past. That's your truth, so don't hide it. Just move on." He was like a saint to me when he said that.' B pauses for a second. 'That is the power of a Hero. That is why I'm a fan. That is why you show your fan-ism to a Hero.' This time, the tone changes. It's confident; he's made all the right moves.

Checkmate.

The interview ends soon. He confesses that his goal in life is to encourage new writers and directors within the Telugu film industry, as long as they write stories only for the Heroes coming from Chiranjeevi's family. Nothing more, nothing less. He gets another call. This time he has to pick it up. He has to sit through another story narration to see if it's worthy of the Hero he manages.

The casino must keep running. The gamblers gamble. The owners of the casino tilt the odds in favour of the house. The dealer shuffles the cards. There are many losers and winners, but *this* dealer has hit the jackpot. Except, he wasn't aiming for the money or the stars. He just wanted to stay in the casino longer than everyone else.

CUT TO
INT. HOSTEL ROOM – DAY

Krishna and his friend nervously walk around in their hostel room. Krishna holds a packet of cigarettes. They are waiting for someone to knock on the door.

FRIEND
Are you sure we won't get caught?

KRISHNA
Stop saying bad things.

We won't get caught.

They hear a knock on the door. They are scared at first. Krishna slowly opens the door and a Telugu weekly magazine that covers cinema gossip juts out of a hand. Krishna takes the magazine and places a packet of cigarettes on the empty palm. The deal has been made. Krishna opens to the page where there has been a report on Actor Krishna's personal life. He has had a son and has named him Mahesh Babu.

KRISHNA
Mahesh. What do you think?

FRIEND
Nice name. Modern.

Krishna smiles. He takes a scissor and begins to cut the article to paste into a book.

CUT TO BLACK

I See Ink

M and B – despite their differences and imperfections – share the similarities of thousands of fans across Andhra Pradesh, Telangana, and wherever else the Telugu films are being watched. Maybe we – the outsiders – will never understand what goes through their head when they see their favourite Hero. It will still seem irrational and silly. For non-fans, the actions of fans are a waste of milk, time, and youth – all precious resources.

In the future, there may be a policy prescription that ensures that young men never gravitate towards such influences and make better use of their time. If our educational institutions offered more holistic learning experiences and ample respect to non-technical courses, there would exist fewer fans of the Telugu Heroes and more writers, historians and actors. Psychologists will perhaps tell us that these young men need a positive male role model in their lives and Heroes play this part. Those fans who crumble with societal expectations of earning money for the family and raising one, find that the role of the 'fan' they play to be the one exceptional space in life where they can be purely selfish. There's a good chance that all this devotion from fans will boil down to boys and their fathers being able to communicate with each other in a healthy manner.

The fan of the Telugu Hero is a curious species. Externally it appears as if the Hero and his family are the sole benefactor of this relationship and like a parasite, the Hero feeds off hapless young men, using their money, time, youth and internet data. But the fan uses the Hero too – to meet his personal end. It might help to think of the Telugu Hero like the Rorschach test that forces the viewer to interpret an image, and the interpretation says more about the viewer than about the image. Similarly, the Telugu Hero is whatever the fan wants him to be – a guide, a distraction, a soothing balm in troubled times, a paternal figure, a portal into an alternate reality.

When you see a 'crazy' fan, pouring milk over a giant cut out of a Hero, the accurate question is, *but why?* But the answer doesn't begin with the charisma of the Hero or his acting capabilities, or even the socio-political responsibilities of the Hero. The answer lies in the personal life of the fan. The casual audience of a Telugu film are accepting and indifferent to every Hero in that they ride the success and abandon him during the flops. But the fan stays through thick and thin. The fan is the one who is loyal beyond the results of the film, because to the fan it is not about the Hero. It's about himself. The fan who pours milk on a cut-out is doing it for himself – either because he wants to feel the power of the sacred or because he wants to see the way milk drops from thirty-five feet. Perhaps he is questioning our idea of God. *You see God in a statue; I see it in this man on celluloid. Who is more irrational?* Whatever his reason, the Telugu Hero will live as long as the Telugu fan finds a use for him. If he doesn't, like the Rorschach painting, the Heroes are just ink and colour with makeup.

CUT TO
INT. HOUSE – DAY

Krishna and his wife hold their baby boy in front of the priest. It's the Hindu naming ceremony of the child, and the priest has suggested the syllable 'ma' or 'mu' for the baby boy. Krishna has known the answer for nearly two decades.

KRISHNA
Are you sure you want to name him that?

WIFE
Listen, if you say Mahesh, one more time, I will leave this baby here and walk out.

KRISHNA
But my name is Krishna, and I'm a fan of Krishna.
His son got 'ma' and now my son got 'ma'.
This was meant to be.

WIFE
I don't care. I've told you what I think.

Krishna looks at his wife, dejected. Then at the baby. He turns to the priest.

KRISHNA
Fine. Name him *Mukesh*.

CUT TO BLACK

6

Vijayashanthi: The Whore, the Madonna, a Hero

'She wasn't a woman who smiled and said hello.'
—Arundhati Roy, *The Ministry of Utmost Happiness*

Shani and Shanthi

My first encounter with Vijayashanthi, the Telugu superstar-turned-politician, was marked by childhood hate. Every summer vacation, my parents, exhausted by our never-ending demands, would parcel me and my younger sister off to the homes of the relatives scattered across South India. This pilgrimage would begin in Hyderabad, where we were subjected to hyper-energetic cousins; their bored parents; dimly lit multi-cuisine restaurants that smelled of burnt garlic and rotis; and film cities that catered to those with weak wallets and non-existent passports, who couldn't make it to Disneyland. Then, we visited our extended family in Bangalore, the city that gave us our first glimpse of adult vices—trails of cigarette smoke that lingered on the street, the sound of satisfied burps from accruing beer bellies, and even the alluring scent of filter coffee from cups nestled in the hands of adults.

Once the cities were done, we'd be packed away in red public transport buses that took us into the insides of Andhra Pradesh and its hot and dusty towns. The experience developed in us a masochistic tendency to eat excessively spicy food that had us in tears, with fresh curd as the only remedy. This annual summer pilgrimage always ended in a small town wedged between the borders of Andhra Pradesh and Karnataka—Pavagada. It was a town of childhood dread, not in the least because of our dislike of the relatives who lived there, but also because Pavagada was a town of extremes. During the day, it felt like the sun would never set, and during the night, it felt like the sun would never rise again. The town worships an unconventional Hindu god—none of the avatars of the holy Hindu trinity, no sir; this non-descript town of childhood trauma worships *Shani*—the god of bad luck and justice. This decrepit acropolis is built around a god who rides crows.

The people of Pavagada, proud Kannadigas, will be offended if they are mistaken for being Telugu, although like a peninsula, the town is surrounded by Andhra Pradesh. However, they see no hypocrisy in appreciating the Telugu films with great zest. There is almost always a Kannada film playing in one of the three single-screen theatres in the town, but the theatre is almost always empty. Instead, people throng the theatres playing Telugu films, or the temple of Shani, the latter probably to seek forgiveness for cheating on the film industry of their mother tongue.

The biggest event in this town's history unfolded because of the love they showered on a Vijayashanthi film, *Osey Ramulamma* (1997). In the film, she plays a Dalit woman who joins the Naxal movement to fight against an oppressive feudal lord who raped her when she was a teen. An earnest police officer sent to curb the Naxal movement finds himself siding with the cause of Ramulamma, and in the end, aids her in extracting revenge. The anti-establishment film played in the same theatre for nearly a year; this was so tectonic in the history of Pavagada that Vijayashanthi herself descended to the small town to visit. A town with an unusual god found an unlikely hero. *Osey Ramulamma* was so successful that the next year, Vijayashanthi joined active politics, transforming from a star into a hero. Even Pavagada, a town that fervently dislikes the language she performs in, began idolizing Vijayashanthi as a 'Hero'.

Over time, I refused to visit Pavagada and instead attended internships and visited friends in more cosmopolitan areas. My Kannadiga relatives, too, had shifted to Hyderabad seeking greener pastures, but they continued watching only Kannada channels at home. Since then, the people of Pavagada have begrudgingly enjoyed many Telugu films, while stone-facedly putting up with mediocre Kannada films.

The last time I visited Pavagada was in the winter of 2018. I wanted to watch a Telugu film in a theatre, *Arjun Reddy*, the film that gave birth to a new star in the pantheon of Telugu cinema. There were new speakers, plush chairs, and a new generation of film-goers. And yet, two decades after Vijayashanthi's visit to Alankaar Theatre, the photos from this visit continue to adorn its walls. Like the god Shani, Vijayashanthi has found her spot in the town of Pavagada.

A Seventeen-Year-Old in Today's India

The year 1983 was special in the history of united Andhra Pradesh. Two heroes were born. First, NTR was sworn in as chief minister for the first time on 9 January that year. After having reached almost god-like status on the silver screen following a three-decade career, this deity stepped out to convert his image into political capital. His nine- month campaign preceding the swearing-in ceremony felt like a script that NTR would star in.

A superstar who had made a career out of playing gods, demi-gods, and mythical beings decided to enter politics as a response to his people being humiliated at the national level. The then chief minister of Andhra Pradesh, T. Anjiah, was apparently reprimanded by Rajiv Gandhi, the Congress general secretary, at the Begumpet Airport in Hyderabad.[3] Capitalizing on the state's wounded Telugu pride (*atma gouravam*), NTR launched his political party, aiming for the highest seat in office. While for most people, establishing a political party requires years of sustained effort, for NTR it seemed almost an impulsive decision. Following nine months of aggressive campaigning, the people rewarded him with the topmost seat in the state. Just like that, he walked over from his throne on-screen to the chief minister's seat, and he took on the most popular leader in India at that time—Indira Gandhi. An insulted people had made their voice heard through their hero.

In October that year, another hero was born. Since the film industry had lost a hero to politics that year, it was time for the Telugu people to find a new one. In contrast to the nepotism that marks the industry today, a hero could emerge from anywhere in the '80s. Chiranjeevi, a constable's son, became an overnight hero after starring in one of the best masala potboilers that year—*Khaidi* (Prisoner; 1983). It was the biggest hit yet in Chiranjeevi's career. With Rambo-like action sequences, the film featured a smouldering Chiranjeevi, who would use guns to deliver revenge to a feudal landlord. His use of ammunition could put entire infantries to shame, and even though he killed his nemesis, he ended up a prisoner, a kaidi. The film posed a larger existential question: was he the prisoner or was it the audience that failed to question the system? He seemed to be saying that those watching him on the silver screen were imprisoned, and only he could lead them to liberation.

---

3   Kidwai, Rashid *Ballot: Ten Episodes That Have Shaped Indian Democracy*. Excerpt can be found on *The News Minute* article titled 'How NTR convinced Indira Gandhi that strong states did not mean a weak Centre,' 5 April 2018.

The '80s were angry times for the Telugu state. It is no coincidence that in that decade, the chief minister changed seven times, the most in any decade.[4] This is despite the fact that the last decade involved the sudden demise of a loved chief minister, Y.S. Rajasekhar Reddy, and the bifurcation of the state. Much of the anger could be attributed to rising unemployment in urban areas. As an increasing number of young men left behind seasonal employment in rural areas and turned to cities, chronic unemployment escalated in Andhra Pradesh's urban areas, at a much faster rate than in the rest of the country.[5]

An iconic depiction of unemployment in the state was the opening sequence of Kamal Hassan's *Aakali Rajyam* (Kingdom of Hunger; 1981), which shows multiple graduates begging with their convocation hats serving as begging bowls. The protagonist of the film, J. Ranga Rao, quotes the Marxist poet Sri Sri and captures young people's disillusionment with the idealism of a post-independent India. An honest but angry upper-caste graduate, unable to find a job, becomes a barber, much to the disappointment of his orthodox father, a classical musician. Worse yet, the most naïve of Ranga Rao's friends becomes a beggar, while the most cunning becomes wealthy after marrying a widow for the property she owns.

A poem of Sri Sri's masquerades as a song in *Aakali Rajyam*. The song is titled 'O Mahatma, O Maharshi', and it captures the spiritual confusion of the decade. It is loosely translated thus:

O Mahatma, O Saint,
Which is light, which is darkness
Which is life, which is death,
Which is virtuous, which is sin,
Which is paradise, which is hell,

---

4   AP State Portal. (Official Portal of Government of Andhra Pradesh).

5   Parthasarathy, G. and Anand, Jayashree. 'Employment and Unemployment in Andhra Pradesh: Trends and Dimensions', *Economic and Political Weekly*, 5 April 1995.

Which is truth, which un-truth,
Which is temporary, which is eternal,
Which is one, which is all,
Which cause, which is effect,
O Mahatma, O Saint.
Which is white, which is black,
Which is a song, which is silence,
Which is mine, which is yours,
Which is moral, which isn't,
Yesterday's dream, today's truth,
Today's sorrow, tomorrow's song
One light, one peace,
O Mahatman, O saint.

Along with unemployment and disillusionment, there existed a moral vacuum in the wake of the Naxal movement—still active, was rapidly losing power and was shifting to Orissa and Chhattisgarh (then Madhya Pradesh). The government crushed the movement and both sides committed atrocities that were beyond redemption. In its early years, the movement, which supported peasant agitations and student movements, held some credibility because of the rising anti-incumbency feeling across the state. But as the violence increased, public support dwindled: kidnappings, murders, and obstructions to daily life orchestrated by Naxalites chipped away at any possible sympathies the movement held within the public sphere.[64] The popular imagination, lacking in political heroes and notions of justice, found instant gratification on the silver screen.

In this context, a scrawny seventeen-year-old raised her voice against the state of the country in *Neti Bharatham* (Today's India; 1983). In the film, Vijayashanthi plays a young woman whose circumstances force her into prostitution. The film tells the story of a

---

6   Shatrugha, M., 'NTR and The Naxalites', *Economic and Political Weekly*, 15 July 1989.

do-gooder police officer, a staple protagonist of the 1980s, who saves an oppressed labour colony from the clutches of an evil politician. It is no coincidence that the politician uses the aid of a corrupt doctor, a dishonest lawyer, and a crooked cop—all serving as stand-ins for their respective professions. The film won a Nandi Award (Silver), the state's award for that year's best film, and the Filmfare Award for best Telugu film.

In one of the film's song sequences, Vijayashanthi exhibits the bubbling rage that would later become her trademark. Just before the song plays, it is revealed that she is working in a brothel, and that the police officer who is raiding the establishment is her childhood friend. It's an awkward situation to cut to a song sequence, but the first image of the song is striking. Vijayashanthi lies on the ground, draped in a white saree, with both her arms resting above her head. The camera gaze voyeuristically lingers over her body, accompanied by blaring synth music. A beat later, the lyrics hit:

'Angam dhopidaina Kanna Talli Jeevitham'
Like the life of a mother who's lost her limbs[7]

The camera slowly zooms out, and it reveals Vijayashanthi lying inside the outline of India. And then, the second line of the song begins:

Idhe idhe, Neti Bharatham.
Bharatha Maatha Jeevitham
This is it, this is it, this is today's India.
The life of Mother India.

There are more striking images: Vijayashanthi is shown behind bars, except that the bars too have taken the shape of India. As she walks

---

7   Here *angam* could also imply 'organs' or 'components' of a larger whole.

around, she is unable to move beyond the bars—Mother India is locked within her own confines. Her hands are in handcuffs, and there's a hangman's noose around her neck as she stares into the distance, ignoring her impending death. As the song progresses, she lists the evils plaguing the country—the poor are thrashed at the hands of the powerful, land and property are unlawfully grabbed, and women are molested in broad daylight. All the while, Vijayashanthi watches as an angry spectator, unable to influence the events that are unfolding before her eyes. While the song ends with the youth of the country breaking her handcuffs and the prison bars she's trapped behind, the rest of it peters out into a choreographed sequence, over-staged even for the palate of the times.

In this one sequence, the audience can see the first glimmers of her potential as a hero, ridding society of its evils and rebelling against the oppressive forces that pervade it. The film foreshadows the rise of the seventeen-year-old Vijayashanthi. That song is, ironically, the last song that the poet Sri Sri ever wrote for a film.

Within that single year, a hero fulfilled his promise in politics, a new hero was coronated to take his place, and a revolutionary poet's last use of ink put forward an unexpected candidate for a future hero. But *Neti Bharatham* was not Vijayashanthi's debut. Her real debut was in a meta-Tamil film called *Kallukal Eeram* (1980), where she falls in love with a film star who visits her village for a shoot. In the climax, unable to deal with his rejection, she commits suicide. She was fourteen years old at the time of the film's release. Her Telugu debut was in a far more mainstream film, opposite Superstar Krishna, titled *Khilladi Krishnudu* (1979), in which she romances a star twenty-two years older than her. Both her debuts happened in 1980, and for the next three years, she juggled both Tamil and Telugu films until she eventually moved to the Telugu film industry in 1983.

Like I said, the year 1983 was a special one for Telugu films.

Resistance and Winds from the West

One of the defining characteristics of a hero is that they have something for everyone. They draw you in, and like a sweetshop owner, offer you at least one item that suits you. They throw every acting chop they have at you, as if to say, *you may not like this film, but you will love me in it*. You could belong to any age, religion, caste, or gender—a hero caters to everyone.

Chiranjeevi was notoriously famous for this. In *Jagadekaveerudu Athilokasundari* (1990), his antics with children and a child-like Sri Devi made him popular among children. He was like the uncle who would sneak you an extra ice cream just after your parents chide you for eating too many. In the film, the children pray to a large statue of Hanuman to protect Chiranjeevi, symbolizing every child praying for Chiranjeevi's safety. When Chiranjeevi takes on the system in *Gang Leader* (1991), he represents the anguish of the young and rebellious. Similarly, in *Gharana Mogudu* (1992), when he 'tames' his wife and mother-in- law, it serves as wish fulfilment for thousands of 'henpecked' middle-aged husbands who hoot and whistle at his acts. On the other hand, in *Hitler* (1997), he protects his sisters from the outside world, letting the audience know that he doesn't think all women need to be 'tamed'. In *Rudraveena* (1988), he takes on the plight of the lower castes and rebels against his father. And just when you think maybe he's lost the demographic of fathers, in *Vijetha* (1984), he sacrifices his kidney and passion for a father who has misunderstood him his whole life.

How can you not love such a hero?

Vijayashanthi is no different; but the first time I saw one of her films, I hated her because of how awkward her film made me feel as a ten-year-old, when all I wanted to watch was an India vs Sri Lanka cricket match. The film, *Pratighatana* (Resistance; 1985) was playing on ETV Telugu, and my mother wanted to watch the film, while I wanted to watch the match. A passive understanding was reached that I would be allowed to check the score during the advertisements.

At first, the film lures you in with cuteness. Vijayashanthi is a professor and her husband, played by Chandramohan, is a lawyer. Chandramohan's short build and silvery singsong voice do not invite physical conflict, unlike Chiranjeevi or NTR who look like they could easily get into a brawl and win it. But the film takes a sharp turn when Vijayashanthi gets into trouble with the villain, the demonic Charan Raj. Vijayashanthi is dragged onto the streets and stripped—a re-enactment of the disrobement of Draupadi by the Kauravas in the *Mahabharata*. Much like the Pandavas, the crowd is unable to do anything, and this time, there is no Krishna to save her. Even her lawyer husband cannot use the power of the Constitution to save his naked wife. Eventually, she is draped in a saree, but by then it's too late. The director seems to be telling the audience that in the Kali Yuga of the '80s, even a disrobed and defenceless woman has to fend for herself.

My mother was already tearing up at this point because of Vijayashanthi's plight, but things get worse. When Vijayashanthi resumes her job as a professor, she walks into a classroom where on the blackboard is a naked woman drawn in chalk with her breasts highlighted. Moved to tears, she reminds the students that the organs they've drawn on the board are a part of their mothers' bodies too. She breaks into a song; again, this is an awkward moment to cut to a song, but it's saved by Vijayashanthi's performance and the legendary lyricist Veturi Sundarama Murthy's words:

In this immoral world of Duryodhana, Dusshasana,
Shedding the tears of blood, I write with anger,
The modern Mahabharatha, the Sixth Veda,
A chapter of rape, about the gloom of a maternal heart.

This is the beginning of the song, and as it proceeds, she laments about the decaying moral compass of the times, and the students watch as emaciated spectators. By now, I was squirming in my place, and my mother was completely reduced to tears. As the film reaches its climax, Vijayashanthi meets Charan Raj, now a public representative. She hacks him to death with an axe on stage, with the support of the students, the people (and my mother) behind her. Legal retribution is barely a pinch compared to the revenge she has enjoyed, and it seems that the only way to resist the evils of the political machinery is to turn into a vigilante. *Even* if you're a woman. *Especially* if you're a woman.

The film was one of the most successful films of 1985, and it turned Vijayashanthi into a star. The Telugu film industry had had female superstars before. Audiences thronged to see Savitri, and people were convinced that Sri Devi was not form this planet, but Vijayashanthi's success was different. She had breached territory that was usually occupied by male stars. Only *they* could be angry at the system. Only *they* could clean it. But Vijayashanthi proved that a woman could do it too, while also being a conventional 'woman' in other films. She could dance, fall in love, and be bratty, but in the right film, she could also beat bad guys to a pulp.

Urvasi Sarada, a star heroine from a generation prior to Vijayashanthi, had also taken on the system in a few films. But Sarada, owing to her age and seniority, could not do the other 'heroine' roles that Vijayashanthi did. When Sarada teamed up with a younger star to clean up the system, it was because she was playing a maternal or an elder sister role, but Vijayashanthi could do it alone. It was believable when she did it alone; nothing was more terrifying than Vijayashanthi being wronged.

She won a Filmfare Award and Nandi Award for Best Actress for *Prathighatana*. But a hero like her can't be restricted to only cleaning the system; she can't always be the angry young woman. She has to prove herself in other roles, walking a tight rope between falling in love without looking too cute, making a fool of herself without appearing foolish, playing a village belle without being too rustic, being the urban woman without looking too posh, and more importantly, she has to have that elusive magnetism that makes her stand out on-screen.

In the years that followed, Vijayashanthi acted in many successful films; in *Swayam Krushi* (1987), she acted opposite Chiranjeevi, playing an uneducated woman who pursues her education in her thirties. Her nervousness when she enters the classroom and her awkwardness when students assume that she is the professor was relatable to many women whose educational dreams were cut short by patriarchal forces. She won a Filmfare Award for her performance in this film as well. She then went on to star in other hit films with superstars such as Balakrishna, Nagarjuna, and even Krishna, with the then 14-year-old Mahesh Babu, now a superstar, playing her son.

It's easy to palm off the credit for these films to her male stars or the directors. Anybody but a female hero. But the success of one film, one part that called for a subtle performance with no scope for histrionics, can be credited only to her—*Padamati Sandhya Raagam* (Evening Ragas of the West; 1987), written and directed by Telugu playwright and director Jandhyala, which won the Filmfare Award for Best Film that year. As a director known for his offbeat and humorous films, working with him gave an actor credibility and scope to flex their comedic and dramatic muscles. In an industry obsessed with conferring titles, Jandhyala was given the title of *Hasya Brahma* (God of Humour).

At that time, it was considered odd for Jandhyala to choose Vijayashanthi, not because she could not perform in dramatic moments, but because people wondered whether she could bite into the ripe comedic situations and punchlines that Jandhyala would whip up for her. Every casting decision in this film reeked of foolishness at that time. The film also featured the debuts of two male actors: Sivamani, the drummer, who plays an African American, and Thomas Jane, who would later star in Paul Thomas Anderson's

Boogie Nights (1997). It was clear whose shoulders the film was riding on, given that its two male leads were 'nobodies' in the Telugu film pantheon.

The film narrates the story of Sandhya and her parents, who move to Baltimore to live with her uncle and aunt. Her neighbours, Chris (Thomas Jane) and Ronald (Sivamani), fall in love with her, and she reciprocates Chris' feelings, much to the annoyance of her conservative father. Sandhya and Chris get married against her father's wishes and have a daughter named Sudha. Sandhya's father takes his granddaughter back to India, so that she isn't influenced by the 'winds of the west', as his daughter was. Years later, after Sandhya's father has passed, it is revealed that Sudha resents her father because of what she has heard from her grandfather. Juggling her conflicting allegiances as daughter, wife, and mother, and unable to choose between the cultural east and the liberating forces of the west, Sandhya tries to bring her family together as a tightly knit unit.

While a contemporary viewer may judge the film harshly (and rightly) for its treatment of the African-American Ronald, Vijayashanthi's performance as a liberated young woman is exceptional. She can neither come across as too eager to rid herself of her cultural roots or so meek that she appears to be swayed by the handsome Chris. She must ensure that the choice appears to be her own, while also winning over audience in theatres. Of course, she is amply aided by Jandhyala's lines, but it's still a tightrope walk. In the end, she not only conveys the message that it is acceptable to fall in love, but also pushes the audience to their limits, making them love her even as she falls in love with a white man.

Heroes can do things like that.

Khaki Is a Cape

Like all mainstream film industries in India, the Telugu film industry too has had a tempestuous relationship with police officers. In films, they are depicted as evil henchmen of the political machinery, or as emasculated and disillusioned servants who relish vigilante justice, or worse, as constables and other lower level officers associated with low-brow humour. But again, nothing announces the arrival of a star more emphatically than when they don the *khaki* uniform. This seems to be true across many Indian film industries. Playing a police officer legitimizes the actions of the hero, not just in terms of cleaning up the system, but even in the punishment met out to goons. If the superheroes of the west wear capes, the heroes of Indian films wear *khaki*. When Ajay Devgn played a senior superintendent of police in rural Bihar in *Gangajaal* (2002), it gave his career a certain gravitas. The film laid the foundation for the popularity of his later *Singham* series.

Tamil superstar, Suriya, reached similar levels of stardom in Tamil Nadu after starring as a police officer in Gautam Menon's *Kaaka Kaaka* (2003). Closer home, following a decade of flops, Pawan Kalyan returned as a police officer in *Gabbar Singh* (2012), the official remake of Abhinav Kashyap's *Dabangg* (2010). Even the twist in *Pokiri* (2006), the film that launched Mahesh Babu into superstardom, was about an undercover police officer who takes on the might of the mafia by chipping away at it from within.

While the role of the police officer has converted stars into superstars, it is not a guaranteed recipe for success. Some of the biggest stars have tasted feeble results in implementing the formula. In the film *SP Parasuram* (1994), Chiranjeevi, playing the titular role, teamed up with Sri Devi after their phenomenal success in *Jagadekaveerudu Athilokasundari* (1990). Despite the star power, the film only did average business owing to the clichéd and weak character assigned to Sri Devi, which left audiences disappointed. Rajnikanth's *Naurku Oru Nallavan* bombed in 1991, despite him playing a police officer in the film alongside Juhi Chawla. The Hindi version, titled *Shanti Kranti* (1991), did not generate as much traction as expected.

Thus, while to truly emerge a hero in the Indian film industry, a *khaki* film is a must, it has to be a good one, or audiences will be unforgiving of *any* hero. And it is in this context that *Kartavyam* (Duty), released in 1990, launched Vijayashanthi's career as a hero. Having watched it on lazy weekend afternoons on TV when there was nothing else to do, I was surprised to encounter it in a film studies course in college. With due respect to the professor, it was a boring lecture, and many students were catching up on their sleep. The professor was discussing *that* scene in the 1995 film *Heat*, starring Robert De Niro and Al Pacino. In the scene, the two famous actors sit across a restaurant table and converse, while the rest of the world watches in awe of their performance. Personally, it felt like one of those scenes that, if the professor didn't tell you it was iconic and the actors weren't such deified figures within pop culture, would pass like an ambulance in heavy traffic ... it's important for the time it's within sight, but once it passes, you barely think about it. But what do I know? I was catching up on lost sleep.

The professor was emphasizing on the importance of the hero cop and the villain meeting in a film, and she casually brought up *Karthavyam*, in the same breath as De Niro and Pacino. How did a film I associated with bored weekend afternoons and ETV Telugu end up in a film studies course? Did *Karthavyam* share a link with *Heat*? Maybe it was the inherent bias that films from some places are superior to others, but I found myself asking if the two films were indeed comparable.

In *Karthavyam*, Vijayashanthi plays an honest and idealistic assistant superintendent of police who is transferred to Vishakhapatnam. The character was inspired by Kiran Bedi, the first female IPS officer of the nation, whose integrity had made her a household name. While other female actors had played police officers earlier, they had seemed unrealistic, whereas *Kartavyam* was based on a story that had already captured the imagination of the nation. The name of Vijayashanthi's character in the film was a spin-off from her own name—Vyjayanthi. That's another thing heroes can do—name their characters after themselves. Chiranjeevi's characters are often called Shankar, a reference to his original name; Balakrishna's characters often had some variation of his name in many films.

Karthavyam sets up a dystopic world where a group of protestors unwilling to budge to the traps of a scheming politician are run over in the dead of the night by a speeding bus driven by a drunk driver, orchestrated by the politician and his cronies, a police officer and a lawyer who've set aside their principles for hefty wads of cash. The villains to civil society are often hidden in plain sight, lurking under the umbrella of the government. But this time, the corrupt police officer asks a question that sets up Vijayashanthi's entry: *What if an honest officer comes to town?*

She's shown entering riding a police jeep, but she isn't wearing her uniform yet. She's at some level still *ordinary*; the superhero is still in plain clothes. She's still relatable to the audience, though the film makes it a point to establish her honesty at the get go. When her ageing grandmother demands that a lower-level constable unpack the suitcases and furniture, Vyjayanti replies that she will do it herself, and asks the constable to only do his duty. With this one incident, we know that she is an officer who fulfils her *karthavyam* (duty).

The first time we see her in uniform, it's without the fanfare that marks a hero's entrance in the *khaki* films of today. She is headed to file her papers, but she's stopped by a disillusioned youth who refuses to make way for a police jeep. He tries to pick a fight with her, but she does not respond. Her anger is apparent, but she keeps it in check and heads to the station. The disillusioned or spectating young man is a common feature in Vijayashanthi's films. He doesn't stand for the youth of the country, but for the country itself, which seems to need to see some heroics to believe in the power of the law.

Once she reaches the station, she notices the police station is in disarray, a metaphor for the poor state of affairs in the country. She makes the errant constables swear an oath that they will fulfil their duties. When her immediate subordinate circle inspector, who does not bother to wear his uniform to work, tells her that he can connect her to the who's who of the city, she sets him straight. It's no coincidence that this errant subordinate is played by Charan Raj, the man who tormented Vijayashatni in *Pratighatana* (1985).

Bad guys, like demons in myths, resurface with every avatar of the hero.

In *Karthavyam*, Vijayashanthi is pitted against minister Muddu Krishna and his son, who terrorize the city through their abuse of power. The film is replete with symbolism. The head of a college is forced to leak a question paper in the presence of a photo of Sarvepalli Radhakrishnan, whose birthday is celebrated as Teacher's Day in India. A minor girl who has been raped runs directly to court, not to seek justice, but to find Vyjayanthi—*justice personified*. All the fight sequences are staged in public; a lawyer is paraded on the roads after being handcuffed; and all the songs are ballad-esuqe in their efforts to praise Vyjayanthi. Even the names of the characters have clear symbolism—the villain's son is named Chakravarti or 'emperor'. He is shown as crushing a modern democratic city through his draconian misuse of power, and the name of the girl he rapes is Karuna (compassion).

Unlike the *khaki* films of today, *Karthavyam* compels Vyjayanti to question her own understanding of law and justice. At first, she considers the two the same—that which is in the Constitution must be right. Early on in the film, when she has to arrest her half-brother, she doesn't give weight to the fact that he's a blood relative. If he's committed a crime, she's a police officer first and only then his sister. She's sure of her place in society. She knows her *karthavyam*. But as her faith in the law is tested when it favours the immoral and criminal, she pauses to reconsider her position. When she has to arrest someone whom she likes for assaulting a police officer, she first hears him out. She pauses for the first time to mull over the grey areas that the law reduces to black and white. The just and the lawful are not the same.

The film also marks the coming of age of her as a hero. She watched from the side in *Neti Bharatham*, and took law into her own hands in *Prathighatana*, but now that she's fully enmeshed within the system, she struggles to enforce the law. United Andhra Pradesh too was similarly disillusioned in 1989, one year before the film released. NTR, the state's first political hero, had been ousted for not living up to the dream he had promised. Initially expected to put an end to the political instability, his tenure caused as much instability if not more. As the film progresses, Vyjayanthi loses all that is dear to her—her father, her credibility, her job. And yet, she does not lose her sense of duty; it is only strengthened. While her final piece of advice to the rape victim to marry her assaulter is outright wrong, she manages to convert the non-believers into believers in the government and its servants.

Regarding the film's script, its writer Paruchuri Gopala Krishna said that there were two major changes made to the film after viewing the original footage. The first was the addition of the death of the father and his subsequent importance in the case that is central to the film. The second, more interesting change, involves the 'love story' the police officer has with the character Suribabu. In the initial cut, the love story between them had been a hindrance to the plot, making Vyjayanthi's character appear weaker. To deal with the problem, they reduced the screen time of the love story and instead fleshed out other subplots. That is a luxury even modern heroes do not enjoy—to dispose the love track to make way for the plot. The film, which was made on a budget of seventy lakhs, is supposed to have collected eight crores. It ran for a year, and more importantly, Vijayashanthi bagged the National Award, Nandi Award, and the Filmfare Award for Best Actress that year. By her own admission, after the success of *Karthavyam*, Vijayashanthi started charging around one crore as her renumeration, unheard of for female lead actors. Appropriately, she was conferred the title of Lady Amitabh Bachchan.

In hindsight, I don't think my professor was wrong. *Heat* and *Karthavyam* can be discussed in the same breath. Not because *Karthavyam* has that *one* iconic scene as *Heat* does. Not because *Heat* has the masala tropes that are found in abundance in *Karthavyam*. But because both pack powerhouse performances that are eulogized in the pop culture spaces that they occupy. If there was a textbook, these would be examples for future actors. Except, Vijayashanthi had one over De Niro and Pacino. She was alone. Or maybe I don't know enough about the scene from *Heat*. Remember, I was sleeping when I was taught how to appreciate it.

Through *Karthavyam*, a new hero was born in the Telugu cinema. This hero, like the others, beat up the bad guys, danced to songs, fell in love, and shouldered a film; but for the first time, this hero was female.

Heroes Need Homes

You think you know Vijayashanthi. You can think of her big, expressive eyes. Her symmetric face that could fit into any role and give life to a range of characters and costumes. She could dance. Fight. She had dusky skin, unlike the heroines of today, which made the audience feel like she was one of their own. She acted in big films. Good films. Hit films. Of course, she was perfect.

Perfect, but not complete.

Audiences had never heard her speak in her films. *Literally*. Directors would almost always hire other artistes to dub for Vijayashanthi, usually preferring actors with 'sweeter' voices, like Roja Ramani or Sarita.[8] Vijayashanthi's voice wasn't gruff, rough, or hoarse; it just wasn't the sugary voice that was the norm of the '80s and '90s. Even if you beat up bad guys, you need a sweet voice.

---

8   Ranjan, Hriday, 'Dubbing and The Death of the Telugu Heroine', *Film Companion*, 9 February 2019.

So when she took the plunge into politics, that was the first time people heard her voice—literally and metaphorically. She started off with the Bharatiya Janata Party (BJP), which does not enjoy a stronghold in Andhra Pradesh. In 2004, when it was widely speculated that the Congress would field Sonia Gandhi or her daughter, Priyanka Gandhi, from Bellary, the BJP had an aircraft on stand-by for Vijayashanthi and then president of the BJP, Venkaiah Naidu, so that she could file her papers in in Bellary, giving the campaign in Bellary a superstar face. When the Congress decided against it, the BJP backtracked as well.[9]

Vijayashanthi later formed her own political party, Talli Telangana Party, to spearhead the Telangana movement, which she eventually merged into the Telanganran Rashtra Samithi (TRS). She said the TRS head, K. Chandrashekhar Rao (KCR), is like a brother to her, but she eventually broke away from the party at loggerheads with the same man. In her speeches and interviews now, he sounds almost like a villain from one of her films.

She is now with the Indian National Congress (INC), which has lost its footing in the both the Telugu states. She was elected member of Parliament from the Medak constituency in 2009, the same constituency that Indira Gandhi held until her assassination. The INC was rejected by the people of Telangana in the state elections of 2014, reducing them to only nineteen seats out of 120 seats. Vijayashanthi says that all Telangana people are her family; but barring her husband, she has no family. Her parents passed away before she turned eighteen and she eventually decided not to have children.

While any attempt to objectively judge Vijayashanthi's fluctuating political career would be futile, her collage-like journey comes together as a whole when she explains it herself. In an interview to

---

9   'Vijayashanthi for Bellary', *The Hindu*, 29 March 2004.

Vanitha TV, she stitches together her story and the snippets become a more cohesive whole.[10]

She speaks of her Telangana roots and her reasons for launching a separate Telangana movement in 1998, when it lacked the popularity it later accumulated in the early 2010s. She heard stories as a child from her mother about the life they left behind in Telangana before her family fled to Chennai. The atrocities of the Razakars, the private militia of the Nizam of Hyderabad, who crushed all Communist and peasant rebellions, forced Vijayashanthi's rich grandfather out of their village. They barely took anything with them. She used the Telugu phrase 'kattubatta', meaning with 'nothing but the clothes they were wearing'. She confesses that these stories sowed the seeds of her interest in the Telangana agitation.

After the hit of *Osey Ramulamma,* she grew closer to her 'home'— Telangana. She claimed that Chennai, though she was born there, never felt like one. Even though she was interested only in social service and not in politics, the BJP lured her in with the promise of granting statehood to Telangana. On 26 January 1998, she officially joined the party, with LK Advani and Atal Bihari Vajpayee personally attending the ceremony. After convincing them that she did not want to contest in the elections, she campaigned for them across India. Dubbed and remade versions of her films had become hits in Tamil Nadu and Maharashtra by then, so her face pulled crowds in non-Telugu speaking states too. But when the BJP backtracked on their promises, she felt neglected, particularly after their alliance with TDP. And thus, she launched her own party in 2005, with the mission of securing separate statehood for Telangana.

While she might have overstated the success of her party, she admits that it was expensive to run, and she was unwilling to accept funds from others because it would make her servile to her donors.

---

10   *Vijayashanthi Personal Interview, Chatta Sabhalo Vanitha,* Vanitha TV, 3 September 2013.

Upon popular demand, in her own words, she 'sacrificed her party' for the larger goal of statehood and merged with the TRS. Apparently, K. Chandrashekhar Rao (KCR), the current chief minister of Telangana, promised to treat her like his own sister, but she was later suspended from the party for anti-party activities. She alleges that she was suspended because she was backstabbed by KCR, who restricted the growth of leaders with whom he did not share familial relations. She was treated as Number 2 in the party, and she was slowly pushed away after her big sacrifice. She doesn't mince words when criticizing KCR. When Chiranjeevi launched his party, her co-star of many successful films, people expected her to be cordial in her words about him, but she launched a scathing attack on him for being fickle-minded about the Telangana issue. She also criticized him for thinking that he could replicate the success of NTR. So KCR was obviously not spared after his betrayal.

After quitting TRS, she joined the INC and contested for state elections in the Medak constituency in 2014, but lost to the TRS candidate. In the years that followed, she had serious health complications, because of which she settled for a less aggressive role in politics. In another interview to the news channel TV9 given in October 2018, she said that her final aim was to establish the INC in a position of power in Telangana. After achieving the goal of statehood, she says this is her next big purpose.[11] Her *karthavyam*.

As of October 2019, there are rumours that Vijayashanthi might return home, to join the BJP.

There is a particularly touching moment in this interview, when the interviewer awkwardly asks her why she decided against having children. She appears frustrated at this sudden personal turn after having had to defend the actions of an unpopular INC. Her answer almost sounds like a line from one of her films. She replies that the

---

11   *Congress Leader Vijayashanthi Exclusive Interview*, TV9 Telugu Live, 2 October 2018.

people are her children. If she were to have children, that would make her selfish and distract her away from a grander purpose of serving people.

The interviewer is dumbstruck because she looks earnest. *This woman means it,* he seems to think.

She then adds that once she dies, all her money will be donated to a trust formed in the name of her mother. The one who told her stories of home. And the trust will distribute the money to the poor of Telangana. Something her grandfather would have done if he hadn't fled the state.

The lives of heroes come full circles like that.

Of course, to trust a politician based entirely on the narrative they construct is foolish. Vijayashanthi's political journey may not have been successful in terms of her political victories, and her constant switching of parties may come across as fickle. But one has to concede that her sheer survival is heroic. The other heroes of the Telugu cinema have embarrassed themselves in politics. NTR was beaten with slippers by his own party members and was ousted out of the party by his son-in-law and children. Chiranjeevi lost the respect he once commanded in the popular imagination after merging his party. Following accusations that he allocated seats to the highest bidders, he failed to win even in his home constituency in Palakollu and just about scraped through in the Tirupathi Assembly seat in 2009. Pawan Kalyan's fiery and dramatic speeches exposed his political inexperience and naivete, costing him both the seats he contested in. His party managed to win only one seat in the elections. He has admitted that entering politics was a big mistake. Balakrishna, NTR's son, and a current MLA, has become a much-ridiculed figure in the Telugu politics.

The Telugu voters have unceremoniously rejected heroes when their political campaigns have been disappointing. Their work on-screen may have been promising, but they are held to a different standard in politics. Those who have failed to understand this have ended up becoming political fools.

But while Vijayashanthi may have been naïve, she is not a fool. And that makes her perhaps the only true hero to have come out of Andhra cinema and politics. In January 2020, she returns to the celluloid screen. If rumours are to be believed, she plays Mahesh Babu's mother, a role that she's played before. But this time, when she comes on-screen, she might have to make way for a new superstar. All the claps and the whistles won't be for her. She will have to make her performance be heard and seen in the cramped 'mother' role— almost always a flat two-dimensional character serving to only prop up the male star in the film. Audiences are happy that the hero has finally come home. Telangana may have been her larger purpose in real life, but on reel, anybody who appreciates the Telugu films finds her irreplaceable.

But for the people who have now heard her voice in politics, to see her back on-screen in a reduced capacity will evoke conflicting emotions. Just ask the unlucky people of Pavagada, the Kannadigas who love a Telugu hero and worship the god of misfortune. I want vindication for my childhood trauma, so I'll be in Pavagada when the film releases. For the first time, *voluntarily*.

7

A Hero and a Judge Walk into a Climax

'Lately in a wreck of a Californian ship, one of the passengers
fastened a belt about him with two hundred pounds of gold in
it, with which he was found afterwards at the bottom. Now, as
he was sinking – had he the gold? or the gold him?'
—John Ruskin, *Unto This Last*

I don't know how to end this book, but if it was a film, it would have
a grand climax. Not an action set piece … no. This one would be
set in a court. The final scene being set in the court is a staple of many
Indian films, and so too with the Telugu cinema and its Heroes.

In the final scenes, the court is not just the one in the film. Even the
space where people are watching the film, becomes a courtroom – the
theatre, the living room, the Telugu states, the minds of all those who
can hear the Hero. The Hero is not only defending his own actions,
but also pointing out the flaws of the society. He presents himself as
the morally upright end of a 'duality' of 'good' and 'bad' created by him.
He is telling the audience, 'My actions maybe illegal, but morally, I'm

unquestionable.' If you haven't guessed yet, Heroes can do things like that: make us root for them, while they break the law and question the system. There are grand dialogues, punch dialogues, sweeping statements about society and humanity. Most importantly, the Hero never stutters because he does not have an ounce of guilt – despite what the legal system (or society) thinks of him.

So too with this book.

The Hero would defend himself. He too would fight his case. You be the judge.

CUT TO
THE CLIMAX

A court session is about to begin. The room looks like a cardboard cut-out court designed by someone who has seen courts only in films.

A Hero, whose age is difficult to determine, stands in the witness box. He looks awkward – like ever part of him was put together from different bodies. A lawyer walks up to him, as if he learnt how to be a lawyer only from films.

Despite being accused of many crimes, the Hero has a self-assured smile on his face. The lawyer rummages through his notes before speaking.

LAWYER
My lord, this man can be accused of multiple crimes that worked against the interests of society. This mere man of paint, colour and trickery is a criminal. My first accusation is that he has stolen blatantly from the folk tales of the past. He not only apes the mannerisms of the Heroes in those tales, but also liberally steals elements and stories from the past. For this, he must be punished.

HERO
Tell me sir, do you—

LAWYER
Do you not have anybody to defend you?

HERO
I am capable of defending myself.

LAWYER
But you do not know the law—

HERO
I know I did not commit any crimes; therefore, I know the truth.

The lawyer remains silent.

HERO
I'm going to take your silence to mean that I get to speak. Tell me, sir. Do you know who owns the folk tales?

LAWYER
The authors for some are known. The authors for most are vague.

HERO
These works of art ... to whom do they belong?

LAWYER
Society. At large.

HERO
And am I not a person in this society?

LAWYER
Perhaps. But you cannot take these figures and stories and maim them and add to them what you feel like and what you don't.

HERO
But if the origins of these folk tales are vague and their authors not fixed, it can surely be assumed that these stories have only changed over the years. When I do portray them or change them, I'm only continuing the tradition. What is the second allegation you have against me?

LAWYER
You have been accused of being the cause of depriving literature of it's worth and pillaging the world of literature for stories and writers and passing their work of as your work. The masses think the words you spit are your own words and not those of writers. For that crime, this Hero, must be punished.

HERO
What purpose do stories serve?

LAWYER
My lord, a question as a response to a question—

HERO
The arrogance of these writers has cost them. They think they speak and write in the same language as all of us. But they don't. To know how to write is to know a different language. They only write for those who know their language.

LAWYER
That still doesn't let you off the hook for the crime of stealing.

HERO

I only stole from those who had and gave it those who hadn't. Are those who cannot read books worthy of the power of stories?

LAWYER

But you bend stories for your will, your tickets are expensive—

HERO

Is my crime that writers are not as successful as I was? Would they not have wanted what I have achieved if they achieved the same success?

LAWYER

[fuming and rummaging through his files]
What do you have to say of caste?

HERO

What of it?

LAWYER

Don't act innocent, you scoundrel.

HERO

Need I remind you we are in court—

LAWYER

Don't tell me how to do my job. I don't take instructions from someone who bends society to the interests of his caste. People like you propagate the caste system and ensure the country doesn't move forward.

HERO

Is my crime that I work towards bending a caste into favourable conditions, while others continue to suffer?

LAWYER
Yes.

HERO
Sir, as the upholder of the law, do you agree that the effects of
the caste system prevail in your profession?

LAWYER
Law is blind to caste. In other words, as lawyers we do not see
caste, but—

HERO
What is your caste?

LAWYER
[stunned]
How dare you?

HERO
If we are discussing my caste, and you assume I'm a criminal, I
need to ensure that you are not taking revenge on me because
you have something against my caste.
  Lawyer is silent.

HERO
All right, if you don't want to be specific, I will play your game.
Is it fair to assume that your caste belongs to the higher rungs
of that oppressive system?
  Lawyer nods.

HERO
Is it fair to assume that you're not an exception, but rather the
rule? Many lawyers and judges belong to upper castes and those
that belong to a lower caste are an anomaly. Similarly, in the

countless newsrooms, government offices, political offices, and our multiple chief ministers, prime ministers and presidents have generally been upper caste, and have propagated the interests of their own caste willingly or unwillingly?

LAWYER
Are you suggesting that the prime minister is as much of a criminal as you are?

HERO
I'm saying I'm doing the same thing they are doing. And my work in cinema and politics is at best is a reflection and at worst a distraction. What of the countless upper-caste folks whose work affects the state, the nation and adds to the misery of the oppressed castes? Are they to be free? Are they not guilty? You tell me the law is blind ... but is it also spineless?

LAWYER
[shaken]
You still have another accusation against you, which you surely cannot escape from.

HERO
I'm not escaping. I'm merely proving innocence—

LAWYER
Enough with words. You have a way of crushing women. Under you, they don't prosper. You hog their limelight and confine the meagre roles around you. They must suffer for you to show your Heroism.

HERO
That's not true. There have been exceptions—

LAWYER

Aha! So you do agree they are mere exceptions. That would imply you expect men to be Heroes and women to be subservient.

Hero is silent. Lawyer has a smug smile on his face.

HERO

May I request the court for a glass of water?

Disregarding protocol, lawyer himself hands him the Hero a cup of water. He thinks he has the Hero in a trap and all the niceties are winning the judge over.

HERO

Before I respond to your statement, may I ask you a question?

LAWYER

Proceed.

HERO

Suppose you have a son and a daughter. Your son wins a race by unscrupulous means. And your daughter noticing this tries the same method. Would you encourage her to do the same as your son or would you rather your son mend your ways?

LAWYER

Your Honour, the witness is wasting the court's precious time.

HERO

Lawyers profit from extending the court cases. Not citizens. We Heroes finish our work within two and a half hours. So please answer my question. Would you allow your daughter to cheat or rectify your son?

LAWYER
The latter.

HERO
Now you as a Lawyer believe that Heroes like me wield too much unfair power and negative influence on society? We valorize violence and aggression; brew and spew dialogues that may instigate strong sentiments; espouse medieval values of honour, gender roles, and ideas society. Are those not your opinions on us?

LAWYER
Yes. One Hundred Percent.

HERO
Then why would you want women to be Heroes when Heroes hold this position? Why would you rather not work towards a society that changes us? Not being able to nab the criminal, would you like to abet the crime?
    [hands the glass of water to the lawyer]
    Are there any other crimes I'm supposedly guilty of?

LAWYER
You toy around with the minds of young men who are addicted to you on-screen. Neither do you rectify their behaviour nor put them on course so that they may lead lives that are useful to society. Worse, when their behaviour is abominable, you do not correct them. You would rather use them to retain your star power than be responsible.

HERO
You argue the current crop of youth are being led astray by the likes of me?

LAWYER
Without a doubt.

HERO
But are they the first generation of youth to be led astray?

LAWYER
What do you mean?

HERO
Hasn't the youth of young men been ruined earlier by older men? Haven't young men been part of heinous crimes because they followed the orders of other men? Haven't young men discovered vices that have led to their ruin, across space and time?

LAWYER
How is that relevant to this accusation?

HERO
I suppose you still haven't understood. Do you remember your friends with whom you grew up, who because of aimlessness in their youth, have squandered what could have been a bright future?

LAWYER
I do.

HERO
What were their reasons? For sure it was not me or my kind.

LAWYER
Some loved money, some took heartbreaks too seriously, and some wanted to fight society rather than change it. Few resorted to drugs, gambling, alcohol.

HERO

It's good for a change to not be the cause of the world's problems. There have been youth who have been led astray, who are being led astray, and who will continue to be led down a path harmful to them and society. The causes are many, but the result is the same.

LAWYER
Are you saying it's not your fault?

HERO
I'm saying that if it wasn't me, it would be something else. And even if I do my job and ask them to behave responsibly, there are other ways in which their minds can be played with. They will see what they want to see. The way we treat our young men is a responsibility that should be shouldered by all, is it not? And to put the onus on me is to give me far too much importance. After all I'm only a man of paint, colour and trickery.
Lawyer and Hero face each other like two bulls about to clash. One convinced the other is a criminal; the other convinced he is a man of colour and paint.

LAWYER
My Lord, I have argued. I rest my case.

HERO
I too have given all arguments and evidence to prove my innocence.
They both turn to the judge.

FADE TO BLACK

Acknowledgements

Firstly, let it be known that everybody being acknowledged here is being acknowledged out of my volition. Nobody is forcing me to add their name here. At least most people. The book is the culmination of years of watching Telugu and non-Telugu films. I'd like to thank my grandmother for introducing me to Telugu films and Prasad Sir for introducing me to non-Telugu movies.

The research for this would have been impossible without the help of Chandralatha, Lavanya Gade, Mahesh Koneru, Sreenivas Paruchuri, Jyothi Akka, Rangacharyulu Sir, Solomon Benjamin, Sreekumar and R. Santhosh.

Thanks to 'Pradeep Mathew' (who didn't want me to reveal his real name), Shehan, W.G. Karunasena and Ari for teaching me how to talk about one's own culture without trying to use the biggest words in the dictionary.

An even more special thanks to Reba, Sanjeev, Vicky Shah, Patol Da, Dushyant, Mario and Neel Chaudhuri for teaching me that what may be a Pyrrhic victory to the world could still mean the world to me, and that's all right.

Sincere thanks to the folks at HarperCollins India and MAMI Film Festival, particulalry—Udayan Mitra, Ateendriya Gupta and Shreya Mukherjee.

Special thanks to Nishtha Singh for making the writing better.

Sincere thanks to my sister and all my cousins for being family that could easily be friends.

Gratitude to Manjari, Nitya, Sithara, Arun and Hari, Mongo and Bhatia for being best friends and better friends than me and being friends like family.

Apologies to Miti Shroff who was instrumental during the writing of the book and put up with me till she could. This book and a lot more would be incomplete without her.

Love only for Richa Rungta. No ifs, no buts.

And finally, most obviously, thanks to my parents who are the cause of everything in my life – the ugly, the beautiful and the delightful.

About the Author

Mukesh Manjunath was the winner of the inaugural HarperCollins–MAMI contest for writing on cinema in 2019. He has written for web publications, comedy shows and online streaming platforms. He lives in Mumbai.

HarperCollins *Publishers* India

At HarperCollins India, we believe in telling the best stories and finding the widest readership for our books in every format possible. We started publishing in 1992; a great deal has changed since then, but what has remained constant is the passion with which our authors write their books, the love with which readers receive them, and the sheer joy and excitement that we as publishers feel in being a part of the publishing process.

Over the years, we've had the pleasure of publishing some of the finest writing from the subcontinent and around the world, including several award-winning titles and some of the biggest bestsellers in India's publishing history. But nothing has meant more to us than the fact that millions of people have read the books we published, and that somewhere, a book of ours might have made a difference.

As we look to the future, we go back to that one word— a word which has been a driving force for us all these years.

Read.

Harper
Collins

HARPER
PERENNIAL

HARPER
BUSINESS

HARPER
BLACK

हार्पर
हिन्दी

HarperCollins
Children'sBooks

HARPER
DESIGN

HARPER
VANTAGE

Harper
Sport